STUD[Y] HEALING

— MADE EASY —

WARRIOR NOTES PUBLISHING

STUDY GUIDE
HEALING
MADE EASY

DR. KEVIN L. ZADAI

Please note that Warrior Notes publishing style capitalizes certain pronouns in Scripture that refer to the Father, Son, and Holy Spirit, which may differ from some publishers' styles. Take note that the name "satan" and related names are not capitalized. We choose not to acknowledge him, even to the point of violating accepted grammatical rules.

Warrior Notes Publishing

P O Box 1288

Destrehan, LA 70047

Cover design: Virtually Possible Designs

For more information about our school, go to www.warriornotesschool.com. Reach us on the internet: www.kevinzadai.com

ISBN 13 TP: 978-1-6631-0133-4

ISBN 13 eBook: 978-1-6631-0134-1

DEDICATION

I dedicate this book to the Lord Jesus Christ. When I died during surgery and met with Jesus on the other side, He insisted that I return to life on earth and help people with their destinies. Because of Jesus's love and concern for people, He chose to send a person back to help everyone who will receive that help. He wants everyone's destiny and purpose to be secure in Him.

I want You, Lord, to know that when You come to take me to be with You someday, I sincerely hope that people remember not me but the revelation of Jesus Christ that You have revealed through me. I want others to know that I am merely being obedient to my heavenly calling and mission, which is to reveal Your plan to fulfill the divine destiny for each of God's children.

ACKNOWLEDGMENTS

In addition to sharing my story with everyone through the book *Heavenly Visitation: A Guide to the Supernatural*, God has commissioned me to write over eighty books and study guides. Most recently, the Lord gave me the commission to produce this title, *Healing Made Easy Study Guide*. This guide addresses some of the revelations concerning the areas that Jesus revealed to me through the Word of God and by the Spirit of God during several visitations. I want to thank everyone who has encouraged, assisted and prayed for me while writing this work. Special thanks to my wonderful wife, Kathi, for her love and dedication to the Lord and me. Thank you to my excellent staff for the beautiful job editing this book.

CONTENTS

INTRODUCTION

Jesus, His disciples, and the early church regularly experienced signs, wonders, and miracles. They operated in the gifts of the Spirit and daily ministered healing to the sick. It was their everyday life. After the 2,000 years that have passed, the church should be on fire, and the supernatural should have increased. Yet, we are not seeing the level of healing we should. There is a great need for an awakening in the body of Christ and for us to return to the simplicity of our faith, which is the purpose of the *Made Easy* book series.

The problem is that many modern ministries have strayed from the Lord's original intent and pursued their own ambitions, which has robbed the people of God. We must return to receiving all God's promises in His Word, including healing. God never made a single person sick and is not withholding healing from anyone. The shift must happen on the receiving end. I pray that as you read this title, the Lord will give you grace to receive your healing and empower you to minister to others.

God bless you,

Dr. Kevin L. Zadai

CHAPTER 1

A COVENANT BENEFIT

Bless the LORD, O my soul, And forget none of His benefits; Who pardons all your iniquities, Who heals all your diseases.
—Psalm 103:2–3 NASB

DISCUSSION:

Throughout the Old and New Testaments, God promised healing as a covenant benefit for His people. He has not changed His mind, therefore healing remains a promise for every believer today. It is not enough to be able to quote the Scriptures, so in this book, we will discuss how to apply these truths. We will explore some Scriptures to expand your understanding of healing, so you can receive it in your own life and help others obtain theirs.

The Lord is the one who gives you the benefits so you can receive them. He pardons all your iniquities. The word iniquity means to twist, which refers to the twistedness of your life[1]. In other words, sin is damaging to your life. God pardons and forgives you of all sin and heals *all* your diseases. Healing is provided for every sickness and disease.

- When you have understanding, administering healing is so simple that a child can do it.

- God has already instituted and initiated the process of healing.

1 "H5771 - ʿāôn - Strong's Hebrew Lexicon (kjv)." Blue Letter Bible. Accessed 14 Feb, 2025. https://www.blueletterbible.org/lexicon/h5771/kjv/wlc/0-1/

- When you get to Heaven, you will realize the covenant that God made with His people includes healing.
- Some diseases may seem impossible to overcome in the natural, but you can believe and receive healing supernaturally.
- There will never be a time when healing is impossible.
- Jesus said in Mark 9:23, "All things are possible to him who believes."
- This means there is a way to receive anything you need in this life.
- God wants you to believe for the impossible, knowing that with Him, the possibility is always there.
- It is not always easy to believe because of the spiritual warfare we endure.

KEY POINTS:

- Healing is a covenant benefit that God has provided for His people.
- You must be fully convinced, have faith, and receive from Jesus Christ.
- We must be prepared to receive a miracle from the Lord in every area of our lives.

What does Psalm 103:2–3 teach us about God's nature regarding healing?

____

____

____

____

____

How does spiritual warfare affect our ability to receive healing?

____

____

____

____

____

❖ Romans 12:2:

And do not be conformed to this world, but be transformed by the renewing of your mind, that you may prove what is that good and acceptable and perfect will of God.

- Everything given to us from Heaven is impossible in the natural realm; miracles are only possible with God.
- You may find it easy to believe the Lord for a bicycle or a car, but difficult to believe for healing.
- However, those are all supernatural miracles from God.
- Everything He provides is a miracle.

- If you are trusting in Him for anything, He is your source.
- If you start perceiving everything as coming from Him, you will begin to depend upon Him for everything.
- You will get to where you do not balk at the size or the difficulty of something; you just receive it.

KEY POINTS:

- We must change our mindset so we will not be limited.
- It does not matter how small or great, how easy or difficult your need is, the Lord's provision is a supernatural miracle.

Can you recall a situation where you experienced or witnessed a supernatural provision?

How can renewing your mind (Romans 12:2) help you remove possible limitations you have in your faith?

____
____
____
____
____

How does seeing everything as a miracle change our attitude toward God's provision?

____
____
____
____
____

❖ Acts 10:38 NLT:

And you know that God anointed Jesus of Nazareth with the Holy Spirit and with power. Then Jesus went around doing good and healing all who were oppressed by the devil, for God was with Him.

- Throughout the Bible, God's people believed that He healed all diseases.
- There never was a time when Jesus refused to heal someone who came to Him. He healed them all without turning anyone away.

- The Lord never made anyone sick.
- Many have thought that God makes people sick for a reason, sometimes to teach them a lesson, but Jesus never did that.

KEY POINTS:

- We know Jesus only did His Father's will (John 5:19).
- If the Father taught people lessons through sickness, He would have done so through Jesus.
- Instead, Jesus is the Healer who ends sickness.
- We should all be receiving healing, so there should be an end to disease and illness in our lives.

Why is it important to understand that Jesus never refused to heal anyone?

What does Acts 10:38 tell us about where sickness comes from?

How does knowing that healing is always God's will impact your faith?

JESUS EXPRESSED THE FATHER'S HEART

❖ <u>Hebrews 1:3 NLT:</u>

The Son radiates God's own glory and expresses the very character of God, and He sustains everything by the mighty power of His command. When He had cleansed us from our sins, He sat down in the place of honor at the right hand of the majestic God in Heaven.

DISCUSSION:

God is a covenant God. He sent Jesus, who not only died for our redemption but was stripped naked and beaten for our healing. Hebrews 12:2 states, "Who for the joy that was set before Him endured the cross," which means He went through all that suffering thinking of you. During an encounter with Jesus, He told me that when He was on the cross, He had my picture before Him, and yours, too.

The Lord wants us to prosper in every part of our being—the spirit, soul, and body (1 Thessalonians 5:23). Paul prayed that we would prosper and be in good health, even as our souls prosper (3 John 2). Jesus sacrificed His life on the cross so that we could be made whole in spirit, soul, and body. I saw what He suffered for when I was in Heaven, but I should have already known that. You must constantly dig for the revelation in God's Word like a treasure hunt, and fight for the truth. You must set time apart, pray, and ask God to speak to you.

- Jesus's death and resurrection as the Lamb of God was the ultimate expression of the Father's heart.
- He purchased our lives so we may receive freedom and healing through Christ. In addition to that, Jesus's entire life, leading up to the cross, was an example for us.
- We are called and empowered by the Holy Spirit to do the same works He did (John 14:12).
- We discussed how Jesus ministered healing to all who came to Him, doing what He saw the Father doing (Acts 10:38; John 5:19).
- Jesus lived His earthly life as the Son of Man. He could not operate as the Son of God because He had to come as one of us to redeem us.

- This offends many people, but the truth is that He traded His divinity and considered Himself not equal to God but became a servant (Philippians 2:5–11).
- If Jesus had ministered as the Son of God, He would not have been able to commission us to do the works that He did.

❖ <u>Luke 5:15 NASB:</u>

But the news about Him was spreading even farther, and large crowds were gathering to hear Him and to be healed of their sicknesses.

- During Jesus's earthly ministry, He became popular by word of mouth.
- The crowds who came to see Him grew enormous, and they had to meet outside.
- They were no longer going to the temple or attending the synagogue.
- When God starts to move outside the church building and the established religion, the crowds begin to gather.
- They came to hear His teaching because they heard that they could be healed in Jesus's meetings.
- After a while, He had nothing to do with the Pharisees, so they started to come out to confront Him.
- The religious leaders were jealous. They did not like that Jesus was followed and beloved by many (Mark 15:10).

I AM THE LORD YOUR HEALER

❖ Exodus 15:26 NASB:

And He said, "If you will give earnest heed to the voice of the LORD your God, and do what is right in His sight, and give ear to His commandments, and keep all His statutes, I will put none of the diseases on you which I have put on the Egyptians; for I, the LORD, am your Healer."

- The Lord speaks to Moses after He delivers the children of Israel out of Egypt.
- Many have been confused about this verse, thinking God put diseases on the Egyptians, because of how it is worded.
- God permits certain things to happen. Some circumstances will occur if the Lord does not intervene. Sometimes, He does not step in, and negative situations happen.
- In this case, the Lord is saying that He will not permit the diseases to come upon the children of Israel that were allowed to come upon the Egyptians.
- Many modern religious leaders who are against miracles and healing use Scriptures like this to teach that God puts sickness on people.
- The Hebrew mindset believes everything comes from God and that He permits certain things because He is in control.
- Yet, we know we are dealing with the prince of the power of the air and unclean, evil spirits behind the scenes on the earth (Ephesians 2:2, 6:12).

- Jewish people did not understand spiritual warfare back then and still do not today, unless they are Messianic and Spirit-filled.

- Many Christians also believe that everything (good and bad) comes from God based on this same mindset.

- However, Jesus expressed in John 10:10, "The thief does not come except to steal, and to kill, and to destroy. I have come that they may have life, and that they may have it more abundantly."

- In the New Testament, the gospel message is good news, which declares that Jesus destroyed the works of the devil (1 John 3:8).

- He also gave us authority over demons and told us that whatever we permit will be permitted, and whatever we forbid will be forbidden (Luke 10:19; Matthew 16:19).

KEY POINTS:

- Jesus restored the authority to believers, which was given to Adam and Eve before they fell.

- We must clear up the false doctrine that God makes people sick because He is not the author of confusion and does not lie (1 Corinthians 14:33; Numbers 23:19).

- He has no sickness to give people.

- We live in a fallen world, and it is satan who is the author of disease, along with his demonic army.

What does it mean for God to be our Healer?

Why do some people struggle with the idea that God does not cause sickness?

How does John 10:10 help clarify who is responsible for sickness?

FINAL DISCUSSION:

In Exodus 15:26, the Lord said He is the Healer of the Jewish people, and we can apply this promise in the New Testament as well. Remember that God created us perfect in the beginning, so there was no sickness or death (Genesis 1:26–31). Jesus came as a human being to purchase us back; therefore, through the new covenant, He restored us to the perfection of Adam and Eve before the fall. Through Christ, we have obtained freedom from every enemy, except for physical death, the last enemy He will abolish (1 Corinthians 15:26–28). According to Paul, physical death is the only adversary that has not been eradicated, so we live out our lives for a certain number of years, and then we pass on. Every other victory and benefit has been given to us through the sacrificial blood of Jesus (2 Peter 1:1–4).

The Lord promised the Israelites in Exodus 15:26, "I will put none of the diseases on you, which I have put on the Egyptians." None of the plagues that came upon Egypt touched the area of Goshen, where God's people lived (Exodus 8:22, 9:4). Some claim that plagues did impact the Israelites because certain passages do not mention Goshen. These assumptions are wrong; Exodus 15:26 shows us that these diseases and plagues did not touch God's people in Goshen. He protected them.

What are some practical steps you can take to build your faith for healing?

____

____

____

____

____

How can you help others receive healing?

What was the most impactful takeaway from this chapter?

CHAPTER 2

MAKE AN ADJUSTMENT

Return and say to Hezekiah the leader of My people, "Thus says the Lord, the God of your father David, 'I have heard your prayer, I have seen your tears; behold, I will heal you. On the third day you shall go up to the house of the Lord.'"

—2 Kings 20:5 NASB

DISCUSSION:

Some people are not healed immediately because they need to make an adjustment in their lives. When we are faced with a challenge and choose to synchronize with God's will, we are often shifted into healing. For example, if you forgive someone or get right with the Lord personally, your healing may manifest in connection with your obedience. In this chapter, we will examine a biblical example of this principle through the life of King Hezekiah, whose healing was directly linked to his repentance.

ROADBLOCKS TO HEALING

- **2 Kings 20:1–4 NASB:**

  In those days Hezekiah became mortally ill. And Isaiah the prophet the son of Amoz came to him and said to him, "Thus says the Lord, 'Set your house in order, for you shall die and not live.'" Then he turned his face to the wall and prayed to the Lord, saying, "Remember now, O Lord, I beseech You, how I have walked before You in truth and with a whole heart and have done what is good in Your sight." And Hezekiah wept bitterly.

- When King Hezekiah became fatally sick, the prophet Isaiah told him to set his house in order because he was going to die.

- The king immediately humbled himself, turned to the Lord, and wept bitterly.

- Then, in 2 Kings 20:5 the Lord spoke to the prophet before he could even leave the area, instructing him to return to the king.

- God said that He heard King Hezekiah's prayers and saw his tears.

- God appeared to have changed His mind, yet it was Hezekiah who changed when he humbled himself before the Lord and repented.

- Since he responded appropriately, God restored him.

- That illness was never meant to be a part of his destiny.

- The prophet returned to the king to deliver the second message that God would heal him because Hezekiah aligned his heart with God's will.

- When he heard the words of the prophet, he decided to make the adjustment.

- When a person seeking healing receives correction and repents, sudden changes may occur, as in Hezekiah's situation.

How do we know that illness was never meant to be part of Hezekiah's destiny?

How did Hezekiah's humility and repentance affect the outcome of his situation?

Have you ever experienced or witnessed a situation where a change in attitude, faith, or obedience led to healing or breakthrough?

❖ <u>2 Kings 20:6–7 NASB:</u>

I will add fifteen years to your life, and I will deliver you and this city from the hand of the king of Assyria; and I will defend this city for My own sake and for My servant David's sake. Then Isaiah said, "Take a cake of figs." And they took and laid it on the boil, and he recovered.

- The Lord gave Isaiah natural instructions to heal the ailment that would have cost Hezekiah his life.
- His healing did not come through the laying on of hands.
- Sometimes, people had to do something to express their faith.
- In this case, God healed the king because he repented.
- We must realize when we have to align our hearts to receive healing from God. Offense or unforgiveness often blocks healing from manifesting.

KEY POINTS:

- God does not change His mind, even if it appears that way; breakthrough comes because people adjust.
- God cannot heal certain people of diseases until they remove the roadblocks in their hearts.
- When you pray for others, ask the Lord if there are any corrections that must be made.
- Let Hezekiah's account encourage you, and remember that some adjustments may be necessary to receive healing.

Why is it important to align our hearts with God's will when seeking healing?

In what ways do repentance and faith play a role in receiving a miracle?

Why do you think God used a natural remedy (figs) in Hezekiah's healing rather than an instant miracle?

Have you ever seen healing come through practical steps like medical treatment, lifestyle changes, or acts of obedience?

What are some common roadblocks that might prevent healing?

When praying for others, why is it important to ask God if there are any corrections they need to make?

What can you do today to align your heart more with God's will?

____

____

____

____

____

❖ 2 Chronicles 32:24–26 NASB:

In those days Hezekiah became mortally ill; and he prayed to the LORD, and the LORD spoke to him and gave him a sign. But Hezekiah gave no return for the benefit he received, because his heart was proud; therefore wrath came on him and on Judah and Jerusalem. However, Hezekiah humbled the pride of his heart, both he and the inhabitants of Jerusalem, so that the wrath of the LORD did not come on them in the days of Hezekiah.

- Let's dive deeper into King Hezekiah's story to gain more insights concerning roadblocks to healing.
- This is the same story about King Hezekiah, but this passage mentions that his heart became proud, which brought wrath upon him.
- It does not say God caused his sickness.
- Yet we must understand that we can open ourselves up to the enemy.
- Notice the revelation that pride was involved, which brought a significant roadblock to healing.

- When Hezekiah humbled Himself, then the Lord came through and healed him.

- Understand that Jesus has already done everything needed to provide healing for everyone.

- The Scriptures reveal that He has paid the price, and you will see this reality when you get to Heaven.

- The only enemy He has not dealt with yet is physical death. This simply means that although we have access to healing, eventually we will all die.

- God never has and never will withhold healing from anyone.

- I encourage you to also read Isaiah 38:1–8, which is another passage about the same story but from Isaiah's perspective.

What role did pride play in Hezekiah's situation, and how did it become a roadblock to his healing?

How does this passage demonstrate that sickness does not come from God, but that we can open ourselves up to the enemy?

____

____

____

____

____

ONLY THROUGH JESUS CHRIST

❖ 2 Kings 1:2 NASB:

And Ahaziah fell through the lattice in his upper chamber which was in Samaria, and became ill. So he sent messengers and said to them, "Go, inquire of Baal-zebub, the god of Ekron, whether I will recover from this sickness."

- In this passage, King Ahaziah fell sick.
- Instead of inquiring of the Lord, he sought out a false god to find out if he would recover.
- This is the opposite of what Hezekiah did when he repented and changed the outcome concerning his destiny.
- Our decisions determine our outcome.
- God is not saying His decisions are set in stone concerning unfavorable situations.

- He is a good God.
- Remember that Jesus went around doing good and healing everyone who was oppressed by the devil (Acts 10:38).
- We must realize that we have a choice to discern that Jesus is the one who gives us abundant life; He is not giving us death or sickness (John 10:10).
- Unfortunately, many people, Christians included, still seek answers through witchcraft, as Ahaziah did.
- They may have their palms read or seek other forms of demonic divination.

KEY POINTS:

- When people seek answers through demonic divination, they are laying themselves on a demonic altar and allowing an evil spirit to determine their fate.
- They are not inquiring of God, who has given us a spiritual inheritance through Jesus Christ.
- The only way that we receive from God is through Jesus, not by inquiring of a demon spirit.

What mistake did King Ahaziah make when seeking answers about his recovery, and how did it differ from Hezekiah's approach?

Why is it dangerous to seek answers through demonic practices instead of turning to God?

How does John 10:10 clarify the difference between what Jesus gives (abundant life) and what the enemy brings (death and destruction)?

❖ <u>James 5:14–16:</u>

Is anyone among you sick? Let him call for the elders of the church, and let them pray over him, anointing him with oil in the name of the Lord. And the prayer of faith will save the sick, and the Lord will raise him up. And if he has committed sins, he will be forgiven. Confess your trespasses to one another, and pray for one another, that you may be healed. The effective, fervent prayer of a righteous man avails much.

- If anyone is sick among us, we are instructed to call for the elders of the church.
- Notice it does not say to call the apostle, pastor, teacher, evangelist, or prophet.
- It tells us to call for the elders of the church, and they are to pray over that person and anoint them with oil in the name of the Lord Jesus.
- Then it says God will heal them.
- The truth that we all have the ability to pray for the sick in the name of Jesus urgently needs to be taught.
- James 5:16 tells us to pray for each other for the "effective, fervent prayers of a righteous person avail much."
- Jesus sent out the twelve, but he also sent out seventy others (Luke 9:1–6, 10:1–12).
- Scripture does not specify that the seventy were a specific group of people but just calls them seventy others.

KEY POINTS:

- You cannot eliminate anyone from preaching the gospel or from the signs and the wonders that follow, including healing.
- All believers can minister healing in the name of Jesus Christ.

Why do you think James instructs believers to call for the elders of the church rather than just spiritual leaders like apostles or prophets?

____

____

____

____

____

Why is it significant that Jesus sent out not only the twelve disciples but also seventy others to minister and heal?

____

____

____

____

____

How does this passage challenge the idea that only certain people can pray for the sick? How can you apply this truth in your own life?

____

____

____

____

____

UNCLEAN BECOMES CLEAN

❖ Luke 17:11–14 NLT:

As Jesus continued on toward Jerusalem, He reached the border between Galilee and Samaria. As He entered a village there, ten men with leprosy stood at a distance, crying out, "Jesus, Master, have mercy on us!" He looked at them and said, "Go show yourselves to the priests." And as they went, they were cleansed of their leprosy.

DISCUSSION:

During Jesus's earthly ministry, He walked in a level of power that superseded all sickness and disease, so He was not afraid to touch people considered unclean by society. In the Old Testament, one was not supposed to touch a man of God or a rabbi because it would make them unclean. If someone broke one of the many laws concerning cleanliness, they were considered unclean and had to go through a process of purification outside the camp. For example, in Leviticus 12:1–4, the Lord spoke to Moses, explaining that when a woman gave birth to a boy, she would be unclean for seven days and then could not touch anything sacred or even go into the sanctuary for thirty-three days while she was in a purification process. There were many laws like this, yet Jesus fulfilled and superseded them all.

In Luke 17:11–14, Jesus healed ten men of leprosy, which was a disease so contagious that people who were inflicted with it had to live isolated from the community. Interestingly, when Jesus healed people from conditions that were considered unclean, like leprosy, He told them to show themselves to the priest, as He did with these men. The reason why this is significant is because the priests knew when a person was leprous. After all, those with the disease had to turn themselves in and report to them; they could no longer have contact with the public. When Jesus told them to go back and report their healing, the priests would recognize them and see that they were completely clean. This superseded what was possible and was undeniably supernatural.

- Jesus was not afraid to touch people who had contagious diseases.
- Think about some of the sicknesses people suffer with today.
- Jesus would not be concerned about getting sick and would not hesitate to touch those who needed healing.
- In His day, touching someone considered unclean was forbidden, yet He did it anyway.
- The healing power that came from Jesus was so strong that sickness could not transfer to Him.
- Instead, the power went out from Him and healed people, then He told them to go to the priest to testify.
- This showed those priests and Pharisees that something impossible had just happened.

- Those who received miracles told them that it was Jesus of Nazareth who healed them.

KEY POINTS:

- Jesus did miracles that were beyond imagination, which was a testimony to the religious leaders of the day.
- Jesus called us to do the same works He did and even greater works in His name (John 14:12).

Why was it significant that Jesus told the ten men with leprosy to show themselves to the priests?

How did Jesus's willingness to touch and heal the sick demonstrate His authority over disease?

How does Jesus's approach to healing challenge societal fears and stigmas around sickness today?

____

____

____

____

____

What does this passage teach us about faith and obedience, considering the lepers were healed *as they went* to the priests?

____

____

____

____

____

FAITH IS A CATALYST

❖ <u>Mark 10:51–52 NLT:</u>

"What do you want Me to do for you?" Jesus asked. "My Rabbi," the blind man said, "I want to see!" And Jesus said to him, "Go, for your faith has healed you." Instantly the man could see, and he followed Jesus down the road.

- The blind man was persistent and believed that Jesus was the Messiah.

- He discerned who Jesus was, which is very important in healing.
- In the Old Testament, some prophecies foretold that the Messiah would preach good news and have supernatural manifestations (Isaiah 35:5–6, 61:1–3).
- It is crucial to understand that the blind man received his healing because of his faith in who Jesus was.

Why do you think Jesus asked the blind man, *"What do you want Me to do for you?"* when his need seemed obvious?

____

____

____

____

____

How did the blind man's response demonstrate his faith in Jesus?

____

____

____

____

____

What does Jesus's statement *"Your faith has healed you"* reveal about the role of faith in receiving healing?

____

____

____

____

____

❖ <u>Romans 10:17:</u>

So then faith comes by hearing, and hearing by the Word of God.

- I have gathered over one hundred verses on healing.
- I encourage you to meditate on these faith-building Scriptures in this book.
- Each of these Scriptures that I am sharing with you reveals a truth that you must understand.
- God is healing and bringing correction to people's lives through His power.
- We all must tend to our faith.
- The Lord is full of life and perfect in every way.
- He not only provided healing but also the grace to receive it by faith.
- When healing starts to manifest through you, whether by a word or the laying on of hands, the news spreads that miracles are happening, as it did with Jesus.

- Many people's doctors have given up on them. Others do not have money for care or no longer trust the medical field.
- When they hear about the miracles, they will want to be a part of any kind of prayer meeting or gathering where people receive healing; it will become a hotspot. When people start to get healed, the crowds will increase.

KEY POINTS:

- The fact that there are so many Scriptures on this subject shows you that it is crucial to understand.
- The question is not whether God heals but "Can you receive healing?"

Why is it essential to continually strengthen our faith, especially in the area of healing?

____

____

____

____

____

How can sharing testimonies of healing encourage others to believe and receive their own healing?

____

____

____

____

____

What steps can you take to grow in faith and better receive the healing God has already provided?

____

____

____

____

____

SPREADING FAITH

❖ John 6:2:

Then a great multitude followed Him, because they saw His signs which He performed on those who were diseased.

- Large crowds formed when people saw the signs that Jesus was performing on those who were sick.

- Through my study of God's past moves, I observed that when one person received healing from the Lord, it connected with those who were present.
- This is what happened with the crowds that followed Jesus.
- Revelation clicks inside of a person that they are able to receive.
- They connect where they could not before because they actually watched the miracle happen.
- Then, the faith in the room or in the crowd starts to rise because they witnessed it.

KEY POINTS:

- When someone witnesses another receive their healing, they often start to think, *Well, if it happened for them, it could happen for me.*
- Then, they cross over that bridge of receiving, and the domino effect begins.
- If you read about revivals and healing movements, they did not begin because God simply chose to heal a group of people, although He sometimes does that in His grace and mercy.
- Someone pulled on the gift operating through a minister and received their healing.

How does seeing someone else receive healing help others believe for their own?

What role does faith play in the spread of healing movements and revivals?

Have you ever witnessed or heard of a miracle that increased your faith? How did it impact you?

❖ <u>Mark 2:12 NASB:</u>

And he got up and immediately picked up the pallet and went out in the sight of everyone, so that they were all amazed and were glorifying God, saying, "We have never seen anything like this."

- Here, people witnessed Jesus heal someone, and their faith was built up.
- Understand that God's healing power is always available; He is always willing and able to heal the sick.
- Yet the question is whether or not people have faith to receive.
- Jesus had to address people's lack of faith all the time.
- When the crowds came and saw something happen, faith increased, and it started a flow.
- I long to see God's grace flowing into everyone's bodies to where people are receiving healing.

❖ <u>Acts 3:8–9 NASB:</u>

With a leap he stood upright and began to walk; and he entered the temple with them, walking and leaping and praising God. And all the people saw him walking and praising God.

- Someone received healing from the disciples' ministry.
- After he was healed, he entered the temple, which was the religious area where the leaders did not accept the followers of Jesus.
- They knew that man was unable to walk because they regularly saw him.

- It's funny that he went into the temple and started dancing and leaping where the Pharisees and priests could witness it.
- The disciples used the name of Jesus to heal this person, so it became a testimony.
- The religious leaders realized that even though they had Jesus crucified, they did not get rid of Him.
- The book of Acts is about the believers who were doing the works of Jesus, preaching the same message, and seeing the same results.
- That is what should be happening today.
- We are supposed to be witnessing more healing in our gatherings.

KEY POINTS:

- I encourage you to pray that the church will align with God's move so we can see miracles increase and help more people.
- Remember that if you have meetings and pray for people, it may just take one being healed to start a chain reaction for others to receive.
- They might be at the tipping point of faith to where they can receive. Jesus often addressed faith because it was the catalyst for receiving their miracle.

Why do you think witnessing miracles firsthand, like in Mark 2:12 and Acts 3:8-9, had such a strong impact on people's faith?

Why was it significant that the healed man in Acts 3:8-9 entered the temple, a place where religious leaders rejected Jesus's followers?

How can seeing one person healed create a ripple effect, leading to more people receiving their miracles?

What steps can the church take today to align with God's move and see more healing and miracles?

CHAPTER 3

BE A BRIDGE FOR PEOPLE

The Spirit of the Sovereign LORD is upon me, for the LORD has anointed me to bring good news to the poor. He has sent me to comfort the brokenhearted and to proclaim that captives will be released and prisoners will be freed. He has sent me to tell those who mourn that the time of the LORD's favor has come, and with it, the day of God's anger against their enemies.

—Isaiah 61:1–2 NLT

DISCUSSION:

When I was in Heaven, the Lord showed me how God used people to start a domino effect. He would essentially lean on them to propel them in a particular direction. Like a domino hits the next and the next, before you know it a chain reaction has started. When people witness the miraculous, they start to relate, and that flow begins. Jesus instructed me, "Just be a bridge to people. Be approachable, someone who people can connect with in their faith. Do not look down on them or speak condescendingly to them. Relate to people by talking straight across to them." That is exactly what I did when I came back.

At first, when I came back from Heaven, I did not even fathom that I would someday be in public ministry on such a broad scale; I just spoke to the individuals who the Lord showed me. The idea is that all believers are meant to be equal in ministry. We are all called to be like Jesus, who healed people and, in that process, caused others to receive as well. When they heard that God was healing people through this Man, their faith began to attach, which started the domino effect.

THE APPROACHABLE MESSIAH

❖ John 9:30–33 NASB:

The man answered and said to them, "Well, here is an amazing thing, that you do not know where He is from, and yet He opened my eyes. We know that God does not hear sinners; but if anyone is God-fearing and does His will, He hears him. Since the beginning of time it has never been heard that anyone opened the eyes of a person born blind. If this man were not from God, He could do nothing."

- A man who Jesus healed from blindness showed himself to the priests and Pharisees saying, "We know that God does not hear sinners, but if anyone is God-fearing and does His will, He hears Him."
- Since the beginning of time, no one had ever heard of someone opening the eyes of a person born blind.
- He was the undeniable evidence that God was healing through Jesus.
- The religious leaders taught that to be a holy man of God, you could not be a sinner; you had to be a God-fearing person who obeys the Law.
- The Pharisees were taught that if a person was born with a disease, such as blindness, it was because of the sins of their parents.

- They were confronted with a discrepancy when they encountered the man who was healed.
- People asked Jesus, "Was this condition because their parents sinned or because they sinned?" (John 9:2).
- The truth is if a person was born blind, it could not be their fault because they had not yet done anything.
- Yet, this was the kind of mentality that was being taught.
- The Bible says that no one had ever heard of someone born blind getting their sight, so this miracle was beyond comprehension.
- The man who was healed challenged the religious leaders by saying, "We know that God doesn't hear sinners."
- God used this situation to show the Pharisees, priests, and all the Jewish religious leaders that this man was the Son of God—the Messiah.

Why was the healing of a man born blind such a significant and undeniable miracle?

____

____

____

____

____

How did this miracle challenge the religious leaders' beliefs about sin and sickness?

How did Jesus use this healing to reveal His identity as the Messiah?

How can this passage help us shift our mindset about the connection between sin and sickness today?

❖ <u>**Matthew 8:2–3 NASB:**</u>

And a leper came to Him and bowed down before Him, and said, "Lord, if You are willing, You can make me clean." Jesus stretched out His hand and touched him, saying, "I am willing; be cleansed." And immediately his leprosy was cleaned.

- Jesus was approachable to those who no one wanted to touch.
- We know it was forbidden for a Jewish rabbi to make contact with anyone with leprosy or other such conditions because they would become unclean.
- Touching a leper would require that they leave the camp and be in isolation to see if they had contracted the disease.
- No one wanted to touch a leper—yet Jesus did.
- Jesus did not say, "Be healed," but instead, He said, "Be cleansed."

KEY POINTS:

- "Be cleansed," was beyond what a rabbi could declare.
- Not only was the man healed, but he was also cleansed of the disease.
- When Jesus touched him, He announced that the leprosy was completely gone at that very point.
- This miracle astonished everyone who observed it because it was the opposite of their familiar mindset.

❖ <u>**Luke 8:46–48 NASB:**</u>

But Jesus said, "Someone did touch Me, for I was aware that power had gone out of Me." When the woman saw that she had not escaped notice, she came trembling and fell down before Him, and declared in the presence of all the people the reason why she had touched Him, and how she had been immediately healed. And He said to her, "Daughter, your faith has made you well; go in peace."

- Like a leper, a person with an issue of blood was considered unclean and was not permitted to be around people.
- This woman was not allowed to be there and was not supposed to touch anyone because she would have made them unclean.
- Due to her touch, Jesus would have been forced to go outside the camp and be isolated because of her disobedience.
- However, in faith, she reached out, touched Him, and was healed.
- Instead of Jesus having to go out, she was healed and announced clean.
- He is more powerful than any disease.

Why do you think the leper questioned whether Jesus was *willing* to heal him? How does this reflect how some people struggle with believing God wants to heal them today?

How does the healing of the woman with the issue of blood (Luke 8:46–48) demonstrate the power of faith?

Why was it significant that Jesus acknowledged her touch instead of letting her remain unnoticed?

Why was it significant that instead of Jesus becoming unclean, the woman was healed and declared clean?

____

____

____

____

____

THE YOKE-BREAKING ANOINTING

❖ <u>Luke 4:18–19 NASB:</u>

> The Spirit of the Lord is upon Me, because He anointed Me to preach the gospel to the poor. He has sent Me to proclaim release to the captives, and recovery of sight to the blind, to set free those who are oppressed, to proclaim the favorable year of the Lord.

DISCUSSION:

Jesus was in the synagogue when He read the scroll, which was open to Isaiah. Isaiah prophesied that the Messiah would come and fulfill all of the promises listed there, which we call the gospel (Isaiah 61:1–3). According to the prophets, like Isaiah, the anointing that the Messiah walked in would bring forth all the signs the passage listed. After Jesus read it, He said, "Today this Scripture is fulfilled in your hearing" (Luke 4:21). Jesus commissioned all believers to share the same message and to do the same miracles He did (John 14:12). He transferred His authority to us; now it is our responsibility to do His works.

The Spirit of the Lord was upon Jesus because He anointed Him to preach the good news, which is the gospel (Luke 4:18). His message brought good news to the poor, the captives, the blind, and the oppressed, along with a demonstration of God's power. He also preached the year of the Lord's favor, which is a reference to *Jubilee* (Leviticus 25:10)[2]. The year of Jubilee was every fiftieth year when everyone's debts would be canceled, so when Jesus proclaimed, "The favorable year of the Lord," He was declaring freedom from debt. We are the Lord's body, and He has left us with this same ministry.

❖ **1 John 2:20 AMP:**

But you have an anointing from the Holy One [you have been set apart, specially gifted and prepared by the Holy Spirit], and all of you know [the truth because He teaches us, illuminates our minds, and guards us from error].

- The same yoke-breaking anointing of the Holy Spirit that was on Jesus is upon you.
- He has anointed us all.
- The manifestation of the anointing is that the gospel message is preached.
- Good news is shared with people.
- With Jesus, this manifested with those oppressed by demons being set free, blind people receiving their sight, and people being set free from religion so that they no longer had yokes of bondage on them.

2 "H3104 - yôḇēl - Strong's Hebrew Lexicon (nkjv)." Blue Letter Bible. Accessed 20 Feb, 2025. https://www.blueletterbible.org/lexicon/h3104/nkjv/wlc/0-1/

- Jesus told the Pharisees that they were supposed to be removing yolks, but instead, they were putting them on the people, so they were not doing what they were supposed to (Matthew 23:4).

❖ <u>**2 Corinthians 5:20–21 NLT:**</u>

So we are Christ's ambassadors; God is making His appeal through us. We speak for Christ when we plead, "Come back to God!" For God made Christ, who never sinned, to be the offering for our sin, so that we could be made right with God through Christ.

- All believers are Christ's ambassadors who are called to teach and preach the good news.

- We are to preach this same message, which has not changed.

- We are all ambassadors, which means we are sent ones who are representing God.

- Jesus's earthly ministry included preparing His disciples to operate in the anointing He had—to preach the gospel and allow God to confirm His message with signs and wonders.

- The Great Commission has not changed and is not isolated to specific individuals.

Why was it significant that Jesus declared, "Today this Scripture is fulfilled in your hearing" after reading from Isaiah?

How does Jesus's proclamation in Luke 4:18-19 define the purpose of His ministry?

What does it mean for believers to be anointed with the same Spirit that was upon Jesus (1 John 2:20)?

How can we, as Christ's ambassadors (2 Corinthians 5:20-21), actively carry out the same message and works that Jesus did?

If every believer is an ambassador for Christ, how should that change the way we approach sharing the gospel in our daily lives?

ALL BELIEVERS ARE MINISTERS

❖ Acts 6:8 NASB:

And Stephen, full of grace and power, was performing great wonders and signs among the people.

- The modern church has been led to believe that only certain people are supposed to be ministers.
- Many have viewed ministry as a profession.

- Scripture clearly states that all believers are supposed to minister and preach the gospel.
- We are also all supposed to impact the marketplace by working and owning businesses as Stephen did.
- We are not all called to be apostles, like Paul and Peter, but we are supposed to be out there ministering to people.
- In the book of Acts, the church appointed other believers to help serve the widows, orphans, and the hungry so that the apostles could dedicate their time to prayer, fasting, and studying the Word (Acts 6:1–6).
- Stephen was one who was appointed to serve; he was full of grace and performed great wonders and signs among the people.

KEY POINTS:

- The early church had to appoint others to serve the needy so the apostles could spend time seeking the Lord.
- That is how the separation of the apostles came to be.
- At that time, those apostles wrote Scripture and were profoundly used by God.
- Today, we no longer see apostles, prophets, or any of the five-fold writing Scriptures.
- Many New Testament believers who were not apostles helped with their outreaches.
- Today, each of us is called to minister, whether in full-time ministry or the marketplace.

❖ **1 Corinthians 9:14–16 NLT:**

In the same way, the Lord ordered that those who preach the Good News should be supported by those who benefit from it. Yet I have never used any of these rights. And I am not writing this to suggest that I want to start now. In fact, I would rather die than lose my right to boast about preaching without charge. Yet preaching the Good News is not something I can boast about. I am compelled by God to do it. How terrible for me if I didn't preach the Good News!

- Paul was an apostle who had every right to accept a salary for his ministry
- However, he forfeited that right and chose to work.
- He boasted about preaching the good news without charge.
- Paul worked for a living and was still very effective, fulfilling his calling.
- Due to his effectiveness, Paul often ended up in jail.
- We should not allow traditional views on ministry to block us or keep us from doing what God has called us to do.

FINAL DISCUSSION:

In college, I had the opportunity to go into full-time ministry. Yet the Lord told me, "No, I want you to go to work at Southwest Airlines." I thought I had disqualified myself because I was returning to a secular job; we were not taught properly about ministry in the marketplace. God still wants us to heal the sick, but He also wants them to be healed out in public. He wants us to prosper and preach the gospel at work. True ministry is not limited to a pulpit.

When I was working, other employees and passengers would often encounter the anointing that was on my life, and it was not something I was consciously doing. I was simply working at seven or eight miles high, doing my job; I would pray in the Spirit and study when I could. I did everything that I still do now; nothing was different. Back then, I did not have a public ministry like I do now, but it was ministry to the people I encountered, which was hidden. People would just come and start talking to me while I was working, then they would encounter the Lord.

Once, as a lady walked by me to go into the restroom by my galley, the plane shifted from turbulence, and she accidentally bumped me. It was not hard; she just brushed against my arm. This lady was not saved and was not a very lovely person, but she was a professional businesswoman. When she touched me, I could feel something go off me onto her. She felt it, looked at me in shock, then started shaking and crying. She did not know what was happening to her, but the anointing had gotten on her. The holiness and fear of the Lord impacted her, so she started to shake and cry. I grabbed her hand and said, "The Lord is calling you to Himself and wants you to turn to Him. Pray with me." I prayed the sinner's prayer with her, and she got saved; I never saw her again.

Similar situations, like what happened with the lady who bumped me, occurred with many different individuals at my workplace. They encountered the anointing of the Spirit of the Lord on me, and I was not on TV yet and did not have a book.

KEY POINTS:

- Everyone can operate the same way.
- We are called to be a bridge for people to encounter the Lord.

- Stephen was a table server who operated by demonstrating notable miracles, and he was not a part of the fivefold.
- You have the same anointing and power.
- You must be fully convinced and see that you are also part of this great commission.
- You do not have to necessarily be a part of the fivefold ministry.
- You can minister healing and every aspect of the gospel to those on your job, family, and community.

How does Stephen's example in Acts 6:8 challenge the idea that only certain people are called to minister?

What does Paul's decision to work while preaching the gospel teach us about balancing ministry and career?

How can believers impact their workplace or community with the gospel, even if they are not in full-time ministry?

____

____

____

____

____

What does it mean to be a "bridge for people to encounter the Lord," and how can you apply this in your daily life?

____

____

____

____

____

How can understanding that all believers are ministers change the way you approach sharing your faith with others?

____

____

____

____

____

CHAPTER 4

EXPRESS YOUR FAITH

When He entered the house, the blind men came up to Him, and Jesus said to them, "Do you believe that I am able to do this?" They said to Him, "Yes, Lord."

—Matthew 9:28 NASB

DISCUSSION:

There has never been a time when the Lord was unwilling to heal someone. However, He does wait for people to express their faith. Remember in Matthew 8:2–3 when the leper said to Jesus, "Lord, if You are willing, You can make me clean." He replied, "I am willing; be cleansed." He sometimes challenged those He healed to demonstrate their faith by showing themselves to the priest. In other passages, the Lord simply assured the person that He was willing and then asked, "Do you believe?"

In different situations where people needed healing, Jesus waited for them to respond. He never said, "I'm not willing," or turned anyone away. Yet He always wanted them to express faith. In this chapter, I will share one of the secret keys the Lord pointed out to me. When Jesus sent me back from Heaven, He showed me why He took specific actions when He healed people.

DISCERNING THE MESSIAH

❖ <u>Matthew 9:27–30 NASB:</u>

As Jesus went on from there, two blind men followed Him, crying out, "Have mercy on us, Son of David!" When He entered the house, the blind men came up to Him, and Jesus said to them, "Do you believe that I am able to do this?" They said to Him, "Yes, Lord." Then He touched their eyes, saying, "It shall be done to you according to your faith." And their eyes were opened. And Jesus sternly warned them: "See that no one knows about this!"

- Jesus was always willing and able.

- At times, that was enough; He would just heal the sick.

- There were other times when Jesus needed the person to show an expression of faith, like with these two blind men.

- The key is that Jesus needed to hear from them to create the connection between what the Father wanted to do and what that person needed.

- They needed to make a connection by faith.

- Jesus wanted people to respond in a certain manner, expressing their faith.

- The two blind people connected to Him with faith and were healed.

- Another secret in this passage is that the men say, "Have mercy on us, Son of David."

- In the natural realm, Jesus was considered the son of a carpenter (Mark 6:3).

- His father's name was Joseph, even though we know that Jesus did not have an earthly father because the Holy Spirit impregnated Mary (Luke 1:35).
- However, His mother, Mary, married Joseph, which is why they called him son of a carpenter.

❖ <u>Isaiah 9:6–7 NASB:</u>

For a child will be born to us, a son will be given to us; And the government will rest on His shoulders; And His name will be called Wonderful Counselor, Mighty God, Eternal Father, Prince of Peace. There will be no end to the increase of His government or of peace, On the throne of David and over His kingdom, To establish it and to uphold it with justice and righteousness From then on and forevermore. The zeal of the LORD of hosts will accomplish this.

- David was not Jesus's earthly father.
- People called Him the Son of David because the Bible prophesied that the Messiah would come through the line of David.
- Psalm 89 says that David would always have someone seated on his throne.
- The Jewish people knew that when the Messiah came, He would be a descendant of David and that He would sit on his throne as King.
- The key is that when people called Jesus the Son of David, they acknowledged He was the Messiah.
- Many times, the people who sought Jesus for healing, deliverance, or whatever they needed, cried out, "Son of David, have mercy on me."

- This phrase was a sign to Jesus that they discerned Him as the Messiah, the Anointed One, which was the expression of faith that Jesus needed.

❖ **Acts 3:16 NLT:**

Through faith in the name of Jesus, this man was healed—and you know how crippled he was before. Faith in Jesus's name has healed him before your very eyes.

- After Jesus ascended to Heaven, throughout the book of Acts, the apostles and disciples used the name of Jesus when ministering healing to people.
- When the authorities questioned how they were doing this, they answered, "In the name of Jesus."
- They were ordered not to speak in that name any longer, yet they continued to do it anyway, obeying God rather than people (Acts 5:40).
- They acknowledged when a person was healed that it was by the name of Jesus.
- When we pray for people or command healing to manifest, we always do so in the name of Jesus.
- Today, as it was the book of Acts, the name of Jesus is the point of contact, the connection with faith, by which people receive healing.

❖ **Matthew 14:34–36 NASB:**

When they had crossed over, they came to land at Gennesaret. And when the men of that place recognized Him, they sent word into all that surrounding district and brought to Him all who were sick; and they implored Him that they might just touch the fringe of His cloak; and as many as touched it were cured.

- When people would confess Jesus as the Messiah or the Anointed One, or when they cried out, "Have mercy on me, Son of David," He responded to their faith.
- Another expression of faith that connects a person with God's healing power is reaching out to touch Him.
- Every person who reached out and touched Jesus's cloak was cured.
- They had to connect to Him by faith.
- That is also what happened with the woman who had the issue of blood.

KEY POINTS:

- Just as she received healing by touching the hem of Jesus's garment, those who touched His cloak were all healed.
- Jesus did not lay hands on them, but virtue still came out from Him. I believe we will see more of these kinds of miracles in our day, too.

Why did Jesus sometimes require an expression of faith before healing someone, as seen in Matthew 9:28?

____

____

____

____

____

What is the significance of people calling Jesus the "Son of David," and how did it demonstrate their faith in Him as the Messiah?

____

____

____

____

____

How does Acts 3:16 show the power of faith in Jesus's name when ministering healing?

____

____

____

____

____

How can believers today express their faith in a way that connects them to God's healing power?

____

____

____

____

____

Why do you think touching Jesus's cloak was enough to heal people, and how does this relate to how we approach Him in faith today?

____

____

____

____

____

THE LORD GOES WITH YOU

❖ Matthew 28:19–20 AMP:

Go therefore and make disciples of all the nations [help the people to learn of Me, believe in Me, and obey My words], baptizing them in the name of the Father and of the Son and of the Holy Spirit, teaching them to observe everything that I have commanded you; and lo, I am with you always [remaining with you perpetually—regardless of circumstance, and on every occasion], even to the end of the age.

- Before I was known as a minister, the Lord used me at work and other places.
- If you want to be promoted, I encourage you to let the Lord work with you where you are.
- Do not make excuses like, "Well, if I had a pulpit ministry, I would be established and have an opportunity to minister to people."
- That is just not the way that it works.
- You must let the Lord use you where you are, knowing that the anointing is already available.
- The anointing to heal is within every believer because the Holy Spirit is within us all (1 John 2:20); He is the one with the power to heal.
- Wherever you go, whatever you do, you are taking the Lord with you.
- You have a ministry.
- We must get out of the mindset that we have to be in a specific mode and have certain things to be a minister.
- We are already established in Christ; therefore, we already have the message with the signs and wonders following those who believe and preach that message (Mark 16:17–18).
- The point is that God confirms His Word, so there is no reason to wait.

- We should be built up in the Spirit and with the Word of God, so we should expect God to move.
- Everywhere I go, I always watch to see if the Holy Spirit is moving and touching people when I am around them.
- I do not always see that happen because of the hardness of people's hearts.
- They are often unaware, so I just go about my business.
- Yet, if I sense a person's hunger or feel that the Lord wants me to say or do something, I will.
- Notice that Jesus did not just go around laying hands on people; they came to Him and asked for help.

KEY POINTS:

- You cannot lay hands suddenly on someone if you do not have that faith connection because they will not be ready to receive.
- However, be open for the Spirit to lead you to those who are hungry and ready.

❖ <u>Mark 6:53–56 NASB:</u>

When they had crossed over they came to land at Gennasaret, and moored to the shore. When they got out of the boat, immediately the people recognized Him, and ran about that whole country and began to carry here and there on their pallets those who were sick, to the place they heard He was. Wherever He entered villages, or cities, or countryside, they were laying the sick in the market places, and imploring Him that they might just touch the fringe of His cloak; and as many as touched it were being cured.

- A person who wants to receive healing must have hunger or a desire for it.
- They must make an effort toward God and you; that is what happened with Jesus.
- When people heard that He arrived at a location, they would come out to see Him.
- Notice that as soon as Jesus got out of the boat, the people recognized Him and brought sick people on pallets to Him.
- Then, He would pray for them, and people would be healed.
- If you look at these situations where people received miracles in the Bible, you will see that it was either the faith of the person who needed healing or those who carried the person to Jesus.
- For example, four friends lowered a man down through a roof to be healed, and Jesus saw their faith (Mark 2:2–12).
- The Scripture does not say He responded to the man on the bed, but the effort of his friends was enough to display faith; Jesus healed him because that connection was there.
- The expression of faith can either come from the person who needs healing or someone else who cares about them.

KEY POINTS:

- You can be like those four crazy friends and see a miracle happen; God would heal people just because of your faith.

- Warrior Notes empowers people to join together in faith through our School of Ministry and Warrior Fellowships, led by ministry students, that gather in homes worldwide.

What role does faith—either from the sick person or from those around them—play in receiving healing, as demonstrated in Mark 6:53–56?

____

____

____

____

____

How can you apply the truth that "wherever you go, you are taking the Lord with you" in your daily life and interactions?

____

____

____

____

____

HEALING VIRTUE

❖ <u>Matthew 15:21–24 NASB:</u>

Jesus went away from there, and withdrew into the district of Tyre and Sidon. And a Canaanite woman from that region came out and began to cry out, saying, "Have mercy on me, Lord, Son of David; my daughter is cruelly demon-possessed." But He did not answer her a word. And His disciples came and implored Him, saying, "Send her away, because she keeps shouting at us." But He answered and said, "I was sent only to the lost sheep of the house of Israel."

- The Canaanite woman cried out to Jesus, saying, "Have mercy on me, Son of David."
- We see that phrase again.
- It is essential to note that although she was not even a Jew, she proclaimed that Jesus was the Messiah; she was Canaanite.
- She sought help for her daughter, who was demon-possessed, but He did not answer her at first.
- Then, His disciples wanted to send her away. Jesus expressed that He was sent to the Jews—the lost sheep of Israel.

❖ **Matthew 15:25–28 NASB:**

But she came and began to bow down before Him, saying, "Lord, help me!" And He answered and said, "It is not good to take the children's bread and throw it to the dogs." But she said, "Yes, Lord; but even the dogs feed on the crumbs which fall from their masters' table." Then Jesus said to her, "O woman, your faith is great; it shall be done for you as you wish." And her daughter was healed at once.

- Even though Jesus said He was called to Jews, the Canaanite woman was not deterred.
- She asked for the crumbs—she just wanted the leftovers.

- When she said that, Jesus was satisfied that she had faith and granted her request.
- The same thing happened with the centurion (Matthew 8:5–13; Luke 7:1–10).
- Jesus commended this woman and the centurion, stating that they had great faith because they were tenacious and had understanding.
- In other words, they did not give up.
- Notice again that she called Him the Son of David instead of the son of Joseph.
- Her expression of faith was enough for Jesus to heal and respond to her request.

KEY POINTS:

- You can teach people that in order to receive healing, they need to be tenacious, saying, "Lord, I'm not coming to You on my merit, good behavior, or because I give," because you do not approach Him that way.
- You come to Him saying, "Lord, have mercy on me. I'll take anything from you."
- That might not sound pleasing to some people, and they might not think that it is great faith. Yet Jesus granted the Canaanite woman her request.
- She did not come on her own merit but approached Jesus with what little faith she had; it was enough to receive deliverance for her daughter.

❖ **Mark 1:32–34 NASB:**

When evening came, after the sun had set, they began bringing to Him all who were ill and those who were demon-possessed. And the whole city had gathered at the door. And He healed many who were ill with various diseases, and cast out many demons; and He was not permitting the demons to speak, because they knew who He was.

- In the first chapter of Mark, Jesus already encountered the crowds coming to Him; they heard that people would be healed of diseases and that demons would leave if they could get to Him.

- Jesus did not go out and try to find people.

- They knew by word of mouth that healing virtue and authority was on Him.

- If you want God to use you, you must stay in place with Him until He promotes you.

- Strengthen yourself and get built up in the truth; then, God will start to manifest and use you at a certain point.

- Testimonies will spread by word of mouth, and the news will begin to get around. As we discussed, once one person gets healed or delivered, others will hear about it and come to you.

- Their faith will be built up because they have seen and heard what happened, which starts a chain reaction.

- That is how God will promote you, so just remain faithful where you are.

- I encourage everyone to work, even though I know being in the marketplace with ungodly people and situations is a challenge.

- You can also start your own business and minister to your customers.

- Paul had his own business making tallits, which are prayer shawls; they called them *tents* (Acts 18:3).

- People would put these shawls over their heads and pray. Only specialized people could make them, and Paul was certified to do so.

- God could give you a business, which you could use to minister to people.

❖ **Luke 4:40 NASB:**

While the sun was setting, all those who had any who were sick with various diseases brought them to Him; and laying His hands on each one of them, He was healing them.

- When people brought those who were sick to Jesus, He laid hands on each of them and healed them.

- He did not turn anyone away.

- The Scripture does not say that some people got healed and others did not; it says He healed everyone.

❖ **Luke 6:17–19 NASB:**

Jesus came down with them and stood on a level place; and there was a large crowd of His disciples, and a great throng of people from all Judea and Jerusalem and the coastal region of Tyre and Sidon, who had come to hear Him and to be healed of their diseases; and those who were troubled with unclean spirits were being cured. And all the people were trying to touch Him, for power was coming from Him and healing them all.

- This is another passage where Jesus healed everyone who came to Him.

- Those who were sick and troubled with unclean spirits were cured.

- The Scripture says that all the people were trying to touch Him, for "power was coming from Him and healing them all."

- Healing virtue was coming out from Him. Notice that it was not Him; it was coming *from* Him.

- Remember that Jesus laid aside His deity to become a servant.

- He considered equality with God as nothing, and He became a servant of all, according to Philippians 2:5–11.

- The power of God was upon Him to heal people. The key here is that Jesus gave us the same ministry that He had.

FINAL DISCUSSION:

Healing virtue came out from Jesus. That is what happened with a woman with the issue of blood. He was in a crowd, and there were all kinds of people pressing against Him, but He felt virtue leave Him at one point. He asked, "Who touched Me?" The disciples commented that everyone was touching Him. However, He felt that one touch where the power left Him and went into that person. That is how healing operated; people reached out and discerned that God was healing people. When they came in contact, they grabbed hold of that healing virtue. That was an expression of faith.

I want to encourage you not to get set in the ways that you have seen healing ministered because it is going to come back to how Jesus operated. You will get to the place where, like Jesus, healing power will leave you without any effort on your part. You may not even be aware it's happening. Jesus had the healing power on Him, but it was just leaving Him as people reached out in faith. All the people were trying to touch Jesus because power was coming from Him and healing them all, right? It doesn't say that He was laying hands on people; instead, hands were laid on Him as people came in contact with Him. I stress this because that is what we will see in the coming days.

What does the persistence of the Canaanite woman teach us about faith and receiving from God?

____

____

____

____

____

How does Jesus's response to the Canaanite woman demonstrate the importance of recognizing Him as the Messiah?

____

____

____

____

____

What role does healing virtue play in Jesus's ministry, and how does faith activate it?

____

____

____

____

____

How can we prepare ourselves to be vessels for God's healing power in our everyday lives?

____

____

____

____

____

CHAPTER 5

THE KINGDOM OF GOD

But the crowds were aware of this and followed Him; and welcoming them, He began speaking to them about the kingdom of God and curing those who had need of healing.

—Luke 9:11 NASB

DISCUSSION:

In the previous chapters, we studied Jesus's ministry and discussed the keys to why people received healing from Him. Today, we all can see the same results because Jesus said we would do the same works He did and even greater ones. For that to happen, we must understand the way that God operates. The Scriptures give revelation, but it is not always apparent or obvious; sometimes, you must dig. When I spent that time with Jesus in Heaven, I noticed that there was a treasure hunt, as He called it.

Jesus expounded on principles that revealed much more than what was on the surface of a Bible verse. I learned to dig deeper to understand God's truths better and become more effective in this life. After that experience with Jesus, I was given a second chance; I believe the Lord sent me back to make a difference. I realized the teaching He gave me was already in the Bible, but I did not previously see it, as mentioned. I can now see fruit from that encounter and the results of treasure hunting. As He taught me, I am sharing with you that we must look with a magnifying glass into the Word and allow the Spirit of God to explain it to us.

HEALING IN THE KING'S DOMAIN

❖ <u>Acts 1:3 NASB:</u>

To these He also presented Himself alive after His suffering, by many convincing proofs, appearing to them over a period of forty days and speaking of the things concerning the kingdom of God.

- Jesus was given an additional forty days on the earth after He was resurrected and before His ascension.
- When I was with Him in Heaven, Jesus asked me to look at what it was that He spoke on.
- Acts 1:3 says that He went around teaching the kingdom of God.
- Then, Jesus asked me, "If you were given another chance for an extra forty days of teaching, what subject would you choose? Choose wisely."
- He continued, "I chose to teach on the kingdom of God in those forty days."
- If Jesus taught on a subject for forty days before He returned to the Father, it must be crucial.
- In Luke 9:11, we read that crowds were following Jesus, who taught them about the kingdom of God and healed those who needed healing.
- After Jesus talked about the kingdom, miracles and healing of the sick manifested.
- I have noticed that talking about the kingdom produces faith.

- The kingdom is a dominion or domain that has a leader.
- Every kingdom has a king who sits on a throne. The throne is the seat of power, representing that authority.
- The king is the ruler of that whole domain, which has boundaries that can either shrink or expand.
- Throughout history, the goal of kings was to expand their kingdoms so they would have conquests to increase their borders.
- The citizens of a kingdom are called its subjects. Some subjects would be part of an army enforcing the king's domain.
- Their territory was protected by walls around it and by the military who guarded it.
- Kingdoms often had borders and outposts which made up their boundaries.
- It is the same with God's kingdom.

KEY POINTS:

- When you preach about the kingdom of God, you must first realize that God is the King who sits on His throne.
- Psalm 89:14 says, "Righteousness and justice are the foundation of Your throne; Mercy and truth go before Your face."
- Psalm 89 shows that the throne of God has different layers, including righteousness, holiness, and truth, which are His character traits.
- The Lord's angels are His faithfulness, who surround Him.

- There are all kinds of borders and boundaries within His kingdom.
- The King of glory decrees truth from His throne; He speaks with final authority, and what He says is binding.
- One of these truths is that He is the God who heals us.

Why do you think Jesus spent His final forty days on earth teaching about the kingdom of God? How does that emphasize its importance?

How does the concept of a kingdom help us understand God's authority and dominion over sickness and disease? (Think of a king ruling his land—does sickness have a right to exist in His territory?)

In Luke 9:11, people followed Jesus to hear about the kingdom, and healing followed. What does this tell us about the connection between understanding God's kingdom and experiencing His power?

If a kingdom has borders and guards to protect it, what are the "boundaries" of God's kingdom in our lives? How can we expand them?

A king's decree is final and binding. If God has declared healing in His kingdom, why do people sometimes struggle to believe and receive it?

____

____

____

____

____

SPOKEN WITH AUTHORITY

❖ Isaiah 55:11:

So shall My Word be that goes forth from My mouth; It shall not return to Me void, But it shall accomplish what I please, And it shall prosper in the thing for which I sent it.

- Not only has God established truth, He *is* truth.
- The Lord speaks forth His Word from His throne; it returns to Him once it accomplishes what He decreed.
- The whole idea of the gospel is that God has spoken His declarations with a scepter in His hand.
- He extends that scepter, which is a symbol of authority.
- The right hand or arm is a sign of strength in the Bible, so God delivers with His right hand, which is a sign of strength.
- So, He wields a sword, He has a weapon, He has all these different symbolic things in the throne room.

- In the throne room, the Lord's angels are all around Him, some of which make decrees.

- There are all types of creatures around the throne that are beyond anything you have ever seen; some are mentioned in the books of Isaiah, Ezekiel, and Revelation.

- Even the biblical descriptions do not compare to what you actually see around the throne.

- We will never be bored in Heaven because there will always be something new to behold; there is so much activity there.

KEY POINTS:

- Jesus chose to speak on the kingdom of God even after He was raised from the dead and ministered for forty days.

- He could have spoken on anything but decided to teach on the kingdom of God.

- Teaching about the kingdom of God, His attributes, and His authority will establish something in people that helps them receive healing.

- When people understand who God is and that He has the power to restore them, it prepares them for their breakthrough.

❖ Matthew 7:28–29:

And so it was, when Jesus had ended these sayings, that the people were astonished at His teaching, for He taught them as one having authority, and not as the scribes.

- People connected with Jesus because He spoke as a man with authority, unlike the Pharisees.

- The difference between Jesus and the religious leaders was that He had the anointing on Him.

- Jesus is very straightforward when He speaks, and He does not hesitate at all.

- Meeting Him in person changed my personality forever; it was a night and day difference.

- I realized that my character at the time had to change; I needed to be fully convinced concerning who God is.

- I can only help those who want to change, so I do not push the truth onto people.

- If someone does not have the desire to receive from God or me, I cannot help them.

- You cannot force anyone to want God's will or to change; you must allow them to make their own decisions.

- Jesus did not coerce anyone.

- He taught people, and some responded in faith by connecting with Him.

- The attachment was to His authority.

KEY POINTS:

- Jesus is always in complete authority, yet He does not push Himself on people.

- He does not always have His way because of people's free will.

- When I was with Him, I saw that many would miss out on God's will because of their decisions.

- Since 2020, many Christians have stopped following the Lord because of the corruption that was exposed in our government, nation, and in the world.

- They saw that God was not having His way, so they became discouraged and chose to walk away.

Isaiah 55:11 says that God's Word will not return void but will accomplish what He desires. How does this truth impact the way we trust in His promises?

In Matthew 7:28-29, the people were astonished because Jesus spoke with authority. What made His teaching different from that of the religious leaders?

How does understanding God's authority help people receive healing and breakthrough in their lives?

Why does Jesus never force His will upon people, even though He has all authority? What does this teach us about free will and our personal responsibility in responding to God?

How can we, like Jesus, speak and act with confidence in the authority God has given us while still respecting people's free will?

COMMAND "YOU ARE HEALED"

❖ **Matthew 10:8 TPT:**

You must continually bring healing to lepers and to those who are sick, and make it your habit to break off the demonic presence from people, and raise the dead back to life. Freely you have received the power of the kingdom, so freely release it to others.

- When I encountered Jesus in the operating room, it changed me.
- He was very different than how He was presented by the ministries and books I was familiar with.
- When I met Him, I realized that only the Word of God accurately represents Him; that was the only aspect of His character that was not shocking.
- He was everything that He spoke in the red letters of the Bible.
- The descriptions of Him in the Gospels, written by His disciples, were accurate.
- Every other aspect of His personality took me aback.
- He was much stronger than I imagined and spoke with great authority and unwavering confidence.
- When Jesus spoke to me, He did not glance away but looked directly into my eyes.
- He was not afraid of anything.

- He did not doubt and was not even concerned about offending me.
- There was one time when He had to tell me the truth concerning a matter and show me what was happening in that situation.
- He knew it would be painful, but He had to share it.
- He said, "I don't mean to show you this to hurt you. This has to happen, so I must deal with it with you."
- Typically, people feel uncomfortable with confrontation because the other person is likely to respond negatively.
- Many people back off when they should not.
- However, Jesus did not relent; He knew how I would react and addressed the issue anyway because it was necessary.

FINAL DISCUSSION:

It is crucial to understand that sometimes the Lord must confront matters of the heart to lead people to the place of receiving their healing. Jesus is firmly established in the ways of the Father and has an intense passion for the kingdom of God. He will never apologize for God's dominion, His principles, or what He has decreed. He will not amend them to make them easier for us to handle. Jesus wants us to know the truth because it sets us free.

When Jesus went around the countryside and taught on the kingdom, it brought correction to those who heard Him. When I encountered Him, I was profoundly transformed. He did not need to address every issue directly; His personality made it clear that I was misinformed about Him in many ways. I am embarrassed at how deceived I was about specific subjects. The reality of the Scriptures became apparent to me when I was with Him.

Jesus spoke to me about some of my friends and revealed their situations. I realized that they were in my life so that God could use me to influence them. He had planned the impact that I would have on these individuals. There were also certain people who He would send into my life to impact me. What bothered me was that most of the people I knew would not be able to continue; they would miss out because they would not go past a certain point.

A day does not go by where I do not grieve for all of my friends who have not gone on with the Lord. I have known them for many years, so it hurts to know they have not produced fruit. My experience with Jesus shook me and woke me up spiritually. When you see the truth, you cannot erase it or deny it. Once I was shown the reality of my friend's situation, I wanted to win them back somehow, but there was nothing I could do about it. Jesus could not force people to accept the truth; He just continued to preach. I have chosen to do the same.

Jesus preached on the kingdom, and then He healed the sick. People received their healing because of the authority that He spoke with. All of us are supposed to connect with the authority of God and command, "In Jesus's name, you are healed." When the Lord declared, "I am the Lord who heals you," in Exodus 15:26, it was a command that came from His throne. When we announce this, a shift happens in the atmosphere. When authority is released, it impacts the airwaves; people can sense it and connect with the Lord. That is how you see people healed. God desires to move in your life to where you receive healing. Then, you can also teach others to receive as well.

Why is it important to recognize Jesus's unwavering confidence and authority when He speaks? How does this impact how we should approach healing and prayer?

In what ways does the truth of God's kingdom bring correction before it brings healing? Why is correction necessary for breakthrough?

Exodus 15:26 declares, "I am the Lord who heals you." What happens spiritually when we speak and command healing in Jesus's name?

What personal barriers might prevent someone from fully stepping into their authority to pray for healing? How can those barriers be overcome?

CHAPTER 6

RESOLVING DISCREPANCIES

This is why the Scriptures say: Things never discovered of heard of before, things beyond our ability to imagine—these are the many things God has in store for all His lovers. But God now unveils these profound realities to us by the Spirit. Yes, He has revealed to us His inmost heart and deepest mysteries through the Holy Spirit, who constantly explores all things.

—1 Corinthians 2:9–10 TPT

DISCUSSION:

We have been discussing the dynamics of healing in the Scriptures and my heavenly experience with Jesus. It was His personality that influenced me to receive from Him. Many have wondered if supernatural encounters increase a person's faith. The answer is that a divine experience *can* increase your faith if you are able to implement the revelation into your life, yet the encounter alone does not guarantee an increase in faith. We will look at what was happening supernaturally when individuals received their healing.

RETHINKING REALITY

❖ Isaiah 6:1–7 AMP:

In the year that King Uzziah died, I saw [in a vision] the Lord sitting on a throne, high and exalted, with the train of His royal robe filling the [most holy part of the] temple. Above Him seraphim (heavenly beings) stood; each one had six wings: with two wings he covered his face, with two wings he covered his feet, and with two wings he flew. And one called out to another, saying,

"Holy, Holy, Holy is the Lord of hosts; The whole earth is filled with His glory." And the foundations of the thresholds trembled at the voice of him who called out, and the temple was filling with smoke. Then I said, "Woe is me! For I am ruined, Because I am a man of [ceremonially] unclean lips, And I live among a people of unclean lips; For my eyes have seen the King, the Lord of hosts.

Then one of the seraphim flew to me with a burning coal in his hand, which he had taken from the altar with tongs. He touched my mouth with it and said, "Listen carefully, this has touched your lips; your wickedness [your sin, your injustice, your wrongdoing] is taken away and your sin atoned for and forgiven."

- You can encounter something supernatural and not understand it.
- When I have had heavenly experiences, I have felt numb for weeks, months, and even years.
- I was not able to assimilate the revelation immediately.
- When you experience a supernatural event, it is shocking and causes you to reconsider what reality is.
- When God shows us the truth from the other realm, it is often difficult to receive because it means that we must change, like Isaiah did when he experienced the holiness of God's throne room.

- It is quite profound how far we have drifted from God's reality.
- Having a supernatural encounter is not always positive, even though you would think it would be.
- When God shows you a revelation, you do not just see or hear it and then move on; you are responsible for implementing it into your life.
- I have listened to many people's stories about their supernatural experiences, yet not many of them actually changed.
- Some became popular, wrote books, and had TV shows, but the impact seemed to wane; these people faded away.
- You may have wondered what happened to individuals who give powerful testimonies of their encounters with God, who you no longer hear about. Although there are different circumstances, most have to do with spiritual warfare. These people have to deal with the discrepancies between what they experienced with the Lord and what is happening on the earth. When you know God's will and see that it is not being done, the earthly realm can be challenging. Many people cannot deal with this discrepancy.

KEY POINTS:

- My encounters with the Lord were not just for me; they were often instructions on how to help others.
- He showed me what to say and do because He wanted to help many people. Most people who the Lord wanted to help did not receive it, which was very discouraging sometimes.

- When Jesus revealed these individuals' situations, I realized that many people I had relationships with were not going to continue with the Lord to fulfill His greater plans.
- Today, knowing that some people are no longer connected with me hurts and disappoints me the most. The Lord instructed me to let them go, which was difficult for me.

DISCUSSION:

Since God revealed His will to send Jesus in the Scriptures, you would think that the Pharisees, the teachers of the Law, and the priests would discern when He came. They were supposed to be the spiritual leaders, so they should have recognized Him and said, "Here's the Messiah." Instead, Jesus was born where the animals were kept and placed in a manger because there was no place for Him elsewhere (Luke 2:7). The shepherds and angels showed up, but there were no Pharisees or priests (Luke 2:8–20). He faced rejection from the beginning.

When Jesus came into His ministry, you would think by that time, the Pharisees would have recognized Him, invited Him speak, and implemented Him into the temple, but that did not happen. He showed up at the Jordan River with John, who was not a Pharisee or part of the religious system. When John recognized Him and baptized Him, the whole Trinity manifested in one instant (Matthew 3:13–17). The heavens opened, the Father spoke, and the Spirit of God came down on Jesus.

The people you think would receive healing from the Lord are not those who usually have it happen. Notice that Jesus's ministry was launched in Cana at a wedding when His mother pushed Him to perform His first public miracle (John 2:1–11). It did not happen in the temple since the leadership in Israel rejected Jesus. He ministered to people who were not accepted in the synagogues or the temple, such as those who were poor, sick, and demon possessed. They all became brand new converts and disciples.

Why do you think supernatural encounters, like Isaiah's vision in Isaiah 6:1-7, often require people to change their perspective on reality?

Why do some people who have powerful encounters with God struggle to maintain their faith or ministry over time? What role does spiritual warfare play in this?

Why do you think the Pharisees and religious teachers, who were experts in Scripture, failed to recognize Jesus as the Messiah?

How can we be more open to receiving healing and breakthrough in unexpected ways, just as Jesus ministered to those outside the religious system?

What practical steps can we take to ensure that any revelation or encounter with God leads to lasting transformation in our lives?

❖ <u>Matthew 13:54–58 NLT:</u>

He returned to Nazareth, His hometown. When He taught there in the synagogue, everyone was amazed and said, "Where does He get this wisdom and the power to do miracles?" Then they scoffed, "He's just the carpenter's Son, and we know Mary, His mother, and His brothers—James, Joseph, Simon, and Judas. All His sisters live right here among us. Where did He learn all these things?" And they were deeply offended and refused to believe in Him. Then Jesus told them, "A prophet is honored everywhere except in His own hometown and among His own family." And so He did only a few miracles there because of their unbelief.

- The people who knew Jesus as the carpenter's son did not receive from Him.
- When He went to His own hometown, He could not perform many miracles because they did not know Him as the Son of David; they knew Him as the son of Joseph.
- They did not discern Him as the Messiah because they grew up knowing and perceiving Him as just a carpenter's son.
- Jesus could not perform miracles because they were offended and did not receive from Him.
- We need more discussions like this because many wonder why people are not healed.

WE NEED THE FIRE OF GOD

❖ <u>Revelation 3:15–16 NLT:</u>

I know all the things you do, that you are neither hot nor cold. I wish that you were one or the other! But since you are like lukewarm water, neither hot nor cold, I will spit you out of my mouth!

- Many believers are trying to figure out why there are certain times when God performs massive amounts of healing and others when nothing happens.

- The truth is that we have become lukewarm, which must be addressed.

- If we want the fire of God to come back into the church, then someone has to release this information.

- John received this revelation from Jesus on the island of Patmos.

- Jesus was just calling it as it was.

- Until then, there are no records of Paul or the other disciples speaking about being lukewarm.

- When we read the message John received, it is hard to believe the church grew cold after all that Jesus had done.

- Then, He sent out the disciples who became apostles, and the church grew.

- You would think that the church would be on fire when the book of Revelation was written.

KEY POINTS:

- Jesus warned the seven churches through John's letters in Revelation 2-3 that they needed to turn back to the Lord and repent.
- Unfortunately, 2,000 years later, the body of Christ has not changed that much.
- We have grown cold compared to the fiery acceleration the early church experienced.
- As we reflect on what is happening in our church, nation, and world, we must acknowledge that we have strayed.

How does Revelation 3:15-16 challenge believers to evaluate their spiritual temperature? What does it mean to be "hot" versus "lukewarm"?

Why do you think the church, which started with such passion in the early days, eventually became lukewarm? What lessons can we learn from this?

How can we personally and collectively rekindle the fire of God in our lives and churches today? What steps can we take to avoid spiritual complacency?

What practical ways can believers encourage a culture of faith in their communities so that more people can receive healing and experience God's power?

If Jesus were to send a letter to the church today, what do you think He would say about its condition? How would He challenge us to change?

____

____

____

____

____

❖ Galatians 6:7–8 NLT:

Don't be misled—you cannot mock the justice of God. You will always harvest what you plant. Those who live only to satisfy their own sinful nature will harvest decay and death from that sinful nature. But those who live to please the Spirit will harvest everlasting life from the Spirit.

- Although God appears to be mocked by the discrepancies we encounter, His Word says He will not be mocked; we will reap what we sow.
- If a person claims to sow corn, they cannot blame God if it comes up as wheat because God is not mocked.
- Whichever seed that is sown produces its own kind.

KEY POINTS:

- Whatever God has intended and spoken will come to pass; it will not return as something different than He decreed (Isaiah 55:11).

- If you look at a person's harvest, it will not mock God. In other words, it is their responsibility for what comes up, not God's.
- If something undesirable grows, you cannot blame God and say, "Well, I didn't plant that."
- If it sprung up, then that is what you planted.
- The body of Christ must acknowledge that we have grown lukewarm and turn back to the Lord so He can ignite our hearts once again.

THE POWER OF THE HOLY SPIRIT

❖ Acts 1:8 NLT:

But you will receive power when the Holy Spirit comes upon you. And you will be my witnesses, telling people about me everywhere—in Jerusalem, throughout Judea, in Samaria, and to the ends of the earth.

- When I met with Jesus, I noticed that His personality is resolute.
- He is fully convinced of His Father's attributes and desires because He knows Him.
- When He lived on the earth, He only did what His Father told Him to do, which resulted in Him purchasing us back (John 5:19).
- During the time that He ministered on the earth, He operated under the power of the Holy Spirit to show us how to do it.

- We were next in line to do the same works.

❖ **Romans 8:15–16 TPT:**

And you did not receive the "spirit of religious duty," leading you back into the fear of never being good enough. But you have received the "Spirit of full acceptance," enfolding you into the family of God. And you will never feel orphaned, for as He rises up within us, our spirits join Him in saying the words of tender affection, "Beloved Father!" For the Holy Spirit makes God's fatherhood real to us as He whispers into our innermost being, "You are God's beloved child!"

- Jesus fully expected His disciples, including us, to reach out to people and heal them, just as He did.
- The whole idea of the gospel is to instill the truth concerning the Father, His authority, and the kingdom into people so they can connect and receive healing.
- One problem is that people often do not have a good father image.
- People who do receive from God are those who have had a good experience with their father.
- If they did not, it would create issues with receiving because they would not perceive God as a good Father.
- These individuals often feel like they are fatherless, as orphans, which can hinder them from being healed.
- They need the Holy Spirit to supernaturally impart the revelation that they are God's beloved children first.

❖ <u>Matthew 18:3–4 TPT:</u>

Learn this well: Unless you dramatically change your way of thinking and become teachable like a little child, you will never be able to enter in. Whoever continually humbles himself to become like this little child is the greatest one in Heaven's kingdom realm.

- Throughout Jesus's ministry, He always represented the Father and only did what He saw Him doing.
- He wanted to impart that relationship to all His followers.
- Many individuals who were once a part of my life could not go on because they could not receive what they needed from the Father.
- Those who receive healing from God often experience miracles more than once because they have simple, childlike faith.
- They also readily accept the love of God, forgiveness, and other benefits of the kingdom of God.
- They do not have much baggage because they have been crushed by the world and have let it all go.
- People who have experienced the mercy and grace of God in their lives are usually very gracious, merciful, and forgiving.
- They are not critical and are open to getting help.
- I shared my experiences in this chapter because my encounter with Jesus changed me.
- Yet others who have had similar experiences found it difficult to process that because they would have to change.

- Just because someone has an encounter does not mean their faith will automatically increase or their character will change.

- Heavenly visitations are going to bring correction.

KEY POINTS:

- To receive a revelation from the Lord, it must be implemented into your life; you must allow it to transform you, which is not easy.

- The devil will not leave you alone either.

- Many people who started ministries based on supernatural events do not always stay the course because of the warfare.

- They need prayer and help from the body of Christ.

- Great persecution arises when people speak the truth.

FINAL DISCUSSION:

You must allow the Holy Spirit to help you process any discrepancies correctly. That way, you will be able to receive healing because you will realize that God is not withholding anything from you. You must also understand that some will not yet receive the truth because they need to resolve their issues about the Father image of God and forgive others.

Another discrepancy that must be overcome is the competition that results from comparing oneself to others. Most people seem to feel uncomfortable if God favors someone over another. We have a hard time with that because of low self-esteem. Scripture says that we should rejoice with those who rejoice (Romans 12:15). We should be happy when someone prospers because we are all connected in a family together; therefore, if one person prospers, we all prosper. If an individual is healed, we all benefit because we are all tied together.

If someone receives healing and I do not, I do not get offended; I am encouraged that I am next in line. You should not get upset when someone else succeeds or receives something from the Lord. Many people take it wrong and wonder, *Why did this happen for them and not to me?* They compare themselves and do not process it right. Most of the people the Lord spoke to me about during my visitations did not respond correctly. The Lord showed me what He wanted for them, and what would actually happen to them in the future. He warned me that they would not continue with Him, which made me feel like I had lost a family member.

Many people have not gone on because of unresolved discrepancies, yet God had many powerful plans for them. Through Warrior Notes, God has connected me with thousands of new people who are now my friends. The same happened with Jesus; the people you would think would be with Him did not continue with Him.

KEY POINTS:

- You must deal with the issues discussed in this chapter to allow God's favor to come into your life.
- Favor does not come because you deserve it or did something special to get God's attention.
- It will come as a miracle because you receive the mercy and grace of God in your life.

Galatians 6:7-8 says that we reap what we sow. How does this principle apply to both our spiritual lives and physical well-being, including healing?

Why do some people struggle to receive healing or blessings from God, and how does one's perception of God as a loving Father impact their ability to receive?

Romans 12:15 instructs us to rejoice with those who rejoice. How can celebrating others' blessings and healings strengthen our faith rather than cause comparison or discouragement?

How can unresolved issues such as comparison, unforgiveness, or misunderstanding God's favor prevent someone from walking in healing and spiritual breakthrough?

CHAPTER 7

UNCONVENTIONAL METHODS

Then He spit on the ground, made mud with the saliva, and spread the mud over the blind man's eyes. He told him, "Go wash yourself in the pool of Siloam" (Siloam means "sent"). So the man went and washed and came back seeing!

—John 9:6–7 NLT

DISCUSSION:

When Jesus healed people, He sometimes chose unconventional and inconvenient methods. Imagine Jesus spitting on you or putting mud in your eyes; that is what He did. There are also certain ministers, like Smith Wigglesworth, who the Lord used in unusual manners. Wigglesworth punched someone, and their tumor disappeared. God does not always heal in the same manner, so we must allow the Holy Spirit to direct us when receiving and ministering to others. We will examine some Scriptures in the Old and New Testaments where people were healed through unorthodox means.

OUT OF THE COMFORT ZONE

❖ 1 Kings 17:19–24:

And he said to her, "Give me your son." So he took him out of her arms and carried him to the upper room where he was staying, and laid him on his own bed. Then he cried out to the LORD and said, "O LORD my God, have You also brought tragedy on the widow with whom I lodge, by killing her son?" And he stretched himself out on the child three times, and cried out to the LORD and said, "O LORD my God, I pray, let this child's soul come back to him." Then the LORD heard the voice of Elijah; and the soul of the child came back to him, and he revived. And Elijah took the child and brought him down from the upper room into the house, and gave him to his mother. And Elijah said, "See, your son lives." Then the woman said to Elijah, "Now by this I know that you are a man of God, and that the word of the LORD in your mouth is the truth."

- There are several stories of powerful miracles God used Elijah to perform.
- God miraculously multiplied a widow's supply of oil and flour, which saved her, and her son's lives (1 Kings 17:8–16).
- The same lady provided Elijah with accommodations.
- When her son died, she blamed him (1 Kings 17:17–19).
- The prophet stretched himself over the boy and prayed that his life would return to him.
- He miraculously rose from the dead.

❖ **2 Kings 4:32–37 NASB:**

When Elisha came into the house, behold the lad was dead and laid on his bed. So he entered and shut the door behind them both and prayed to the LORD. And he went up and lay on the child, and put his mouth on his mouth and his eyes on his eyes and his hands on his hands, and he stretched himself on him; and the flesh of the child became warm. Then he returned and walked in the house once back and forth, and went up and stretched himself on him; and the lad sneezed seven times and the lad opened his eyes. He called Gehazi and said, "Call this Shunammite." So he called her. And when she came in to him, he said, "Take up your son." Then she went in and fell at his feet and bowed herself to the ground, and she took up her son and went out.

- In 2 Kings, we see a similar miracle but with Elijah's successor, Elisha.
- God used Elisha to perform a miracle for the barren Shunammite woman.
- Then, her son died, and Elisha raised him back to life, just as Elijah had raised the widow's son.
- In the Old Testament, there were only specific individuals who could heal, and the prophet was one of them.

❖ **2 Kings 5:10–14 NASB:**

Elisha sent a messenger to him, saying, "Go and wash in the Jordan seven times, and your flesh will be restored to you and you will be clean." But Naaman was furious and went away and said, "Behold, I thought, 'He will surely come out to me and stand and call on the name of the LORD his God, and wave his hand over the place and cure the leper.' Are not Abanah and Pharpar, the rivers of Damascus, better than all the waters of Israel? Could I not wash in them and be clean?" So he turned and went away in a rage. Then his servants came near and spoke to him and said, "My father, had the prophet told you to do some great thing, would you not have done it? How much more then, when he says to you, 'Wash, and be clean'?" So he went down and dipped himself seven times in the Jordan, according to the word of the man of God; and his flesh was restored like the flesh of a little child and he was clean.

- This is another example of an unusual method of healing.
- Naaman was royalty, so he got angry when Elisha told him to wash in the Jordan River because it was muddy and dirty.
- When he complained and requested to dip in cleaner waters, his servant encouraged him to do what the man of God instructed.
- After he dipped seven times in the Jordan, his leprosy was cured.
- There are not many accounts of miracles in the Old Testament, but the prophets were persistent in their effectiveness.
- They had to get the recipient to participate in an act of obedience to show their faith, even if it was uncomfortable for them.
- From the front row, I witnessed Kenneth Hagin slap a woman who needed healing.
- When her ear popped open, it sounded like a gunshot, but it was not from the physical strike.
- Brother Hagin slapped her hard with a full arm swing, and she was completely healed.
- I have seen miracles like this up close.
- Although we would not have chosen that mode of operation, God can heal people in whatever manner He chooses.

Why do you think Jesus and the prophets in the Old Testament sometimes used unconventional or uncomfortable methods to heal people? How does this challenge our expectations of how God works?

____

____

____

____

____

In 2 Kings 5:10-14, Naaman initially resisted following Elisha's instructions because they seemed beneath him. How can pride or personal expectations sometimes prevent people from receiving healing or blessings from God?

____

____

____

____

____

How can witnessing or experiencing miracles in unexpected ways increase our faith, even if the methods used seem unconventional or uncomfortable?

What lessons can we learn from the persistence of prophets like Elijah and Elisha in bringing healing and miracles? How can we apply that persistence in our own faith journey?

TRANSFERENCE OF POWER

❖ Matthew 10:1 NASB:

Jesus summoned His twelve disciples and gave them authority over unclean spirits, to cast them out, and to heal every kind of disease and every kind of sickness.

- Jesus transferred the same power He had to His disciples, which was unheard of in the Jewish tradition.

- In the Jewish culture, there was an elite group of people who were qualified to minister, such as a rabbi.

- To become a teacher of the Law, a person would have to go through the initiation process in the synagogues.

- They had to go through specific training to become a Pharisee.

- Paul was studying under Gamaliel to eventually become the head Pharisee (Acts 22:3).

- He was striving to be the head of all of the Jewish religion, so he had Christians killed to impress their headquarters, hoping for a promotion.

- Jesus sent forth the fishermen, tax collectors, lawyers, and His other disciples to perform what would be considered a priestly duty.

- Even though the priests did not perform miracles, people came to them to be pronounced clean or healed.

- Jesus was in a class of His own, and the religious leaders could not figure it out.

- It was unheard of for ordinary people to be ordained and sent out to do the same works He did.

- From the perspective of religious people, only priests could minister healing.

- They did not have the power to heal but still felt that miracles should come from them.

- They believed that they were the men of God who the people were supposed to look to.

- Many people are leaving churches today because they are stifled and told, "You're not the pastor here. You're not the spiritual leader. You're just a sheep."

KEY POINTS:

- We are all sheep, even the ministers.
- We are all equal, but God portions out specific assignments to individuals.
- Every believer can and should be ministering healing, not just those in the leadership.

❖ 1 Corinthians 12:22–27 NLT:

In fact, some parts of the body that seem weakest and least important are actually the most necessary. And the parts we regard as less honorable are those we clothe with the greatest care. So we carefully protect those parts that should not be seen, while the more honorable parts do not require this special care. So God has put the body together such that extra honor and care are given to those parts that have less dignity. This makes for harmony among the members, so that all the members care for each other. If one part suffers, all the parts suffer with it, and if one part is honored, all the parts are glad. All of you together are Christ's body, and each of you is a part of it.

- Every member of the body of Christ is essential.
- Paul used the metaphor of a human body needing all its parts to function to demonstrate that we all need each other.
- There is no hierarchy concerning value; the little toe is just as important as the arm.

- If a toe hurts, it will affect the whole body.
- You might not think it is important until it is injured, and you feel the pain.
- Then, you will realize that it matters.
- Jesus gave the twelve disciples His authority without consulting headquarters or the Pharisees, challenging the entire religious system.
- All believers have the anointing and gifts of the Spirit in us. We are all called to preach and are being brought forth.
- People have had enough of being hindered from operating under the power of the Spirit and prevented from being in ministry.
- If you are in a church where the pastor understands that everyone is gifted and anointed, that is great.
- Yet, how many churches and pastors do you know that would allow others to minister?
- Jesus summoned the twelve in Matthew 10:1, giving them authority over unclean spirits.
- All He did was stand there and tell them, "I'm giving you this authority to cast out demons."
- Until then, they had been observing Jesus as He ministered without realizing they would do it themselves.
- They were probably amazed that it worked, like the disciples who were sent out in Luke 10:17.

- They started as spectators, but the day came, and He gave them the authority.
- Jesus gave His disciples the authority to heal every sickness and disease.
- *Every* means they had the authority to cure *all* types of ailments in His name, no matter what.
- Jesus did not give His authority to the Pharisees or the priests.
- He did not minister in the synagogues or the temple but out in the countryside with His disciples.
- The twelve were not qualified in the eyes of the religious organization at the time, yet they went out and saw the manifestation; this was unheard of because they had not attended school or gone through the vetting process.

KEY POINTS:

- Jesus is turning to the ordinary people and the children.
- He is giving them the authority to do His work just like He did.
- He does not work with those who are resisting Him.
- When Jesus spoke to John on the Isle of Patmos, He gave him messages in the form of letters to send to the seven churches (Revelation 2-3).
- Jesus didn't appear to the leaders and pastors of those churches because they were not listening.
- They resisted Him, so He did not speak directly to them.

- He talked to John and asked him to send letters of warning.
- All of those churches, which were in northern Turkey, have disappeared. None of them exist anymore.

❖ <u>**Luke 9:1–2 NASB:**</u>

And He called the twelve together, and gave them power and authority over all the demons and to heal diseases. And He sent them out to proclaim the kingdom of God and to perform healing.

- The twelve became the leaders of God's move, but the Jewish religion was not included.
- Jesus sent His disciples out to preach on the kingdom of God.
- Here you have this subject again.
- That is why everything that we present through Warrior Notes has to do with the kingdom advancing and having dominion.
- We all have the authority and the responsibility to be involved and allow God to manifest Himself; this is a common thread throughout all the things that happened in the early church.

Why was it significant that Jesus gave authority to His disciples, rather than the religious leaders of the time? How does this challenge traditional ideas about who is qualified to minister?

Many people feel unqualified to minister healing or preach the gospel. How does Jesus's decision to empower ordinary people encourage us to step into our God-given authority?

Luke 9:1-2 states that Jesus gave His disciples power over demons and diseases. How can modern believers walk in that same authority today?

Why do you think some churches or leaders resist allowing all believers to walk in the gifts of the Spirit? How can we help encourage a culture where every believer is empowered?

RESISTING THE RELIGIOUS SPIRIT

❖ 2 Timothy 3:1–5 NLT:

You should know this, Timothy, that in the last days there will be very difficult times. For people will love only themselves and their money. They will be boastful and proud, scoffing at God, disobedient to their parents, and ungrateful. They will consider nothing sacred. They will be unloving and unforgiving; they will slander others and have no self-control. They will be cruel and hate what is good. They will betray their friends, be reckless, be puffed up with pride, and love pleasure rather than God. They will act religious, but they will reject the power that could make them godly. Stay away from people like that!

- Jesus's disciples were sent out to preach on the kingdom of God.
- The Pharisees and Jewish leaders were not teaching anything that Jesus taught.
- They were like police officers, making sure that people obeyed the law.
- They enforced the payments of tithes, offerings, and the temple tax, which was not even in the law; that was their idea.
- They invented another way to collect money besides what God had instituted.
- Apparently, the tithes, offerings, and alms were not enough, so they had to invent a tax.
- Religion essentially pressures people to perform.
- It places a demand on them to financially support the system that is enslaving and limiting them.
- When the religious spirit hinders the Spirit of God from moving among the people, healing and miracles stop.
- Many people feel stifled by the religious spirit, just like in the time of Jesus.

- We must expose what is happening and provide a place for people to encounter God, receive healing, and be cared for.

- The church must discern what the Holy Spirit is saying for this time and season.

- We can provide an opportunity for the people who do not fit in with the establishment, just as Jesus did.

- The religion of Jesus's day was not providing for people's needs; it was enslaving them.

- The leaders were ripping the people off by requiring them to show up, sacrifice, and pay.

- Jesus flipped over the tables of the temple money changers because they were defrauding the people.

- The money changers at the temple misled the people concerning the exchange rates.

- They also rejected the sacrificial animals people brought with them, saying they were unacceptable, and forced them to buy their animals instead.

- Then, they took the rejected animals they collected and turned around to sell them to others as acceptable.

- They had a scam business, so Jesus flipped over the tables saying, "The Scriptures declare, 'My Temple will be called a house of prayer,' but you have turned it into a den of thieves" (Matthew 21:13 NLT)!

- John the Baptist called the Pharisees a "brood of vipers" (Matthew 3:7). Jesus addressed them as sons of satan, saying, "For you are children of your father the devil, and you love to do the evil things he does" (John 8:44 NLT).

- Can you imagine if someone spoke that way to denominational leaders today? The church has become cold.

- The Lord says we need to rise to the occasion and provide for those who have been ostracized or left out.

- That is what Jesus did; He went out to the people and served them the way the priests and religious leaders were supposed to.

KEY POINTS:

- God should have been allowed to move and minister to people in the synagogues, but He was not.

- Jesus was their answer, and He gave authority to His disciples so they could perform the same works.

- Imagine how the Pharisees reacted when they found out that not only was Jesus doing miracles, but now these fishermen and common people were doing the same.

- There was proof of Jesus's power and the word spread.

❖ **Acts 3:6–8 NASB:**

But Peter said, "I do not possess silver and gold, but what I do have I give to you: In the name of Jesus Christ the Nazarene—walk!" And seizing him by the right hand, he raised him up; and immediately his feet and his ankles were strengthened. With a leap he stood upright and began to walk; and he entered the temple with them, walking and leaping and praising God.

FINAL DISCUSSION:

Jesus's transference of authority continued in the book of Acts as well. One hundred and twenty disciples were filled with the Holy Spirit on the day of Pentecost. The church grew by three thousand on that same day. Afterward, it continued to multiply and expand. After Jesus ascended back to Heaven, the disciples walked by an area of the temple and ministered healing to a man. Jesus had been there many times, so we can assume this person was there for a while. For some reason, He did not receive healing when Jesus was there, but Peter used the name of Jesus and commanded this man to walk. He walked, leaped, and praised God, so his healing was displayed.

The Pharisees, Sadducees, and priests witnessed an authentic handoff of authority from Jesus to His followers. The public also witnessed these ordinary men perform miracles, which turned the world upside down (Acts 17:6). That will happen again all over the world. We are going to see it before our eyes in the church.

How did the religious leaders in Jesus's day turn faith into a system of control and financial gain? In what ways do we still see this happening today?

Why do you think Jesus and John the Baptist spoke so strongly against the Pharisees? How does this challenge the modern church's approach to religious hypocrisy?

Acts 3:6-8 records Peter healing a lame man in Jesus's name. What does this event teach us about how the authority of Jesus continued through His followers?

Why do you think some people did not receive healing while Jesus was physically present, but later received it through His disciples? What does this reveal about God's timing and faith?

How can the modern church move away from religious control and instead provide a place where people can truly encounter God's power?

CHAPTER 8

INCREASING AUTHORITY

To such an extent that they even carried the sick out into the streets and laid them on cots and pallets, so that when Peter came by at least his shadow might fall on any one of them. Also the people from the cities in the vicinity of Jerusalem were coming together, bringing people who were sick or afflicted with unclean spirits, and they were all being healed.

—Acts 5:15–16 NASB

DISCUSSION:

We discussed the dynamics of God's outpouring in the early church and how we will see that again today. Peter and Jesus's other disciples did not appear to be very bold at first; they were unsure, and it did not seem favorable at times for these men to carry what Jesus was carrying. When the Holy Spirit came, He started producing fruit in these people; many were healed through their ministry. It was displayed among the public that the disciples were doing the same miracles that Jesus did. In this chapter, we will continue to examine how they grew in power and authority.

The move of God in the early church did not stop with Peter ministering healing by laying hands on people. He previously told a man who could not walk, "Silver and gold I do not have, but what I do have I give you: In the name of Jesus Christ of Nazareth, rise up and walk." When he grabbed his hand, the man got up and walked (Acts 3:6–7). Peter's authority continued to increase to where people were being laid on the streets so that his shadow would touch them. Many were healed and delivered from evil spirits through encounters with his shadow.

KEY POINTS:

- Jesus did not always lay hands on people to heal them.
- At times, they just reached out to touch His garment and were all healed.
- After Jesus ascended, the early church grew, and people came from everywhere to be healed.
- It was not Jesus in the flesh anymore, but Him working through the apostles and disciples.
- As you read through the book of Acts, you will notice the acceleration of the church's growth.

❖ <u>Acts 9:32–35 NASB:</u>

Now as Peter was traveling through all those regions, he came down also to the saints who lived at Lydda. There he found a man named Aeneas, who had been bedridden eight years, for he was paralyzed. Peter said to him, "Aeneas, Jesus Christ heals you; get up and make your bed." Immediately he got up. And all who lived at Lydda and Sharon saw him, and they turned to the Lord.

- Peter did not touch Aeneas but simply said, "Get up," which was profound.
- You may not have considered that Peter operated with centurion faith.
- Remember when the centurion soldier said to Jesus, "Just speak the word, and it'll be done," his servant was healed (Matthew 8:5–13; Luke 7:2–10).

- When I met Jesus and observed His personality, the same immovable faith was instilled in me.
- This encounter transformed my life and helped me navigate the challenging times.
- When a person has a supernatural experience, they need grace to deal with the affairs of this life.
- After my encounter, it took many years for my body to recover and for my mind to assimilate what Jesus revealed to me.
- The reality of the truth I was shown vastly differed from what I was taught and was experiencing.
- As we discussed, there is a tendency to be discouraged when you do not know how to deal with the discrepancies.
- Once you encounter the other realm, you realize that Heaven is the real world, and this one appears to be fake.
- Reality seemed to flip on me; this earthly life became a façade, and the other realm became the real world.
- The truth is that the heavenly realm is not always open to us the way it is during a supernatural encounter.
- Someone may have an experience, but it may never happen again.
- When I went to Heaven, I realized I may never see some of what Jesus showed me while still on earth.
- That has been the case in some ways; I have had other visitations, but they were not like the first encounter.

- When you experience something like that, it is not easy to have to live down here.

- Jesus's disciples had to process everything they experienced with Him.

- For some reason, they did not understand that Jesus came to die.

- They misinterpreted all the prophecies concerning the Messiah and thought they were receiving a king who would be with them forever.

- They anticipated that He would physically force Rome out of their land, deliver them from the oppression, and restore their country to them.

- Throughout history, Israel had encountered conquests with Babylon, Persia, and Rome; all those empires enslaved them.

- Jesus's followers thought He would be the one who would fulfill the prophecies of deliverance, but it did not happen the way they expected.

- When Jesus was handed over to the authorities and crucified, His disciples were overcome with discouragement.

- You must understand that they thought God had finally sent the Messiah who would deliver them from Roman oppression.

- Even though Jesus foretold of His death, they still did not anticipate Him being crucified, so it was a huge disappointment.

- It was not until after Jesus rose from the dead and ascended to Heaven that the Spirit of God started to help the disciples become apostles.

- They had performed miracles at the word of Jesus while He was alive, but did not immediately discern that they could do it on their own without Him being there.
- It was nice to have their mentor with them, but then they had to recover from the shock and disappointment of His crucifixion.

KEY POINTS:

- When people encounter the other realm and go into ministry, it can be challenging to function in this realm.
- It is very discouraging when God has revealed His plans, and then it does not happen with the power you expected.
- You would think that others would receive the Lord's revelation with gladness, but they have difficulty accepting the truth.
- Just as Jesus's disciples had to overcome discouragement, those who have encounters today must do the same.
- We read about the progress of His disciples and apostles through the book of Acts and start to see them walk in confidence and boldness.
- The same will happen with you.

Acts 5:15-16 describes people being healed simply by Peter's shadow passing over them. How does this demonstrate an increase in spiritual authority? How can believers grow in authority today?

Peter spoke healing to Aeneas without touching him (Acts 9:32-35). How does this compare to the centurion's faith in Matthew 8:5-13? What does this teach us about speaking with authority in prayer and healing?

The disciples initially struggled to understand Jesus's mission and were discouraged by His crucifixion. How can believers today navigate disappointment when God's plans do not unfold as expected?

The disciples only fully stepped into their authority after Jesus's ascension. What does this tell us about how faith matures over time? How can we step into greater boldness in our walk with God?

OVERCOMING SATANIC ENTRENCHMENT

❖ <u>Ephesians 6:12 AMP:</u>

For our struggle is not against flesh and blood [contending only with physical opponents], but against the rulers, against the powers, against the world forces of this [present] darkness, against the spiritual forces of wickedness in the heavenly (supernatural) places.

- Today, many people do not weather the discouragement of seeing what God had for this nation, yet the corruption embedded in our government has not allowed His will to be done.
- They feel like they have been robbed and are dwelling in a spiritual desert; this is because of the satanic entrenchment that was always here.
- It was there at the time of Jesus, but He just focused on preaching the message of the good news and healing all who came to Him.
- He did not address Rome or come against the government; He even instructed His followers to pay taxes.
- Jesus minded His own business, which was His Father's business.
- The apostles did not come against the government either; they simply preached the good news, and then healing and miracles happened.
- The church should anticipate the needs of the people who are now outside in the marketplace.

- People are not satisfied with going to church. Many still attend services because they feel comfortable there, but for the most part, anyone who understands spiritual reality knows there is more.
- Yet, they do not know what to do about it because they depend on church leadership.
- Too many people do not want the responsibility or accountability, so they do not seek God on their own.
- They do not study the Bible past a certain point but do just enough to appease their conscience.
- Most people work enough to pay the bills and do just enough to feel like they have accomplished something; it is all cosmetic.
- When most people attend church, they want the pastor to feed them and help them spiritually.
- Jesus's great commission to make disciples aims to have them walk in authority and become leaders.
- Jesus mentored the twelve, the seventy, and all of His other disciples, whom the Bible does not name.
- We do not know much about them, but they healed, performed miracles, and cast out demons.
- That is how I view everyone connected to Warrior Notes; we are sending you out into the marketplace to do the works of Jesus.

KEY POINTS:

- The church leadership is doing the work that the individuals are supposed to be doing.
- The Lord instructed me to be a self-feeder.
- I am supposed to feed myself spiritually.
- The pastor is a shepherd who is supposed to lead you to green pastures and still waters, but the sheep are supposed to eat and drink themselves.
- The pastor cannot make you eat or drink; He is supposed to provide a place for you and protect that area.
- Churches are supposed to be places where people can go to worship and have a safe place where they can be served.
- People should be taught and mentored so they can worship the Lord and have communion together.
- Understanding that the demonic realm has infiltrated our systems, so we do not become discouraged in the spiritual battle is crucial.
- Believers must focus on spreading the gospel and healing the sick, like Jesus did.

Ephesians 6:12 states that our struggle is not against flesh and blood but against spiritual forces. How should this understanding shape the way believers respond to corruption, injustice, and opposition in the world today?

Jesus and the apostles focused on preaching the gospel and healing rather than confronting the government. How can modern believers apply this principle while still making an impact in society?

HEARING GOD FOR YOURSELF

- Hebrews 4:14–16 NLT:

So then, since we have a great High Priest who has entered Heaven, Jesus the Son of God, let us hold firmly to what we believe. This High Priest of ours understands our weaknesses, for He faced all of the same testings we do, yet He did not sin. So let us come boldly to the throne of our gracious God. There we will receive His mercy, and we will find grace to help us when we need it most.

- Every sacrifice Jesus made was so that we could personally go into the holy of holies.
- Jesus is our Intercessor, our Mediator between God and people.
- Since the New Testament church, every believer is supposed to hear from God themselves, and the ministry gifts should confirm it.
- God planned to back up what He has personally spoken through the ministry gifts, operating through ordinary people in the congregation.

❖ <u>1 Corinthians 14:26 TPT:</u>

Beloved friends, what does all this imply? When you conduct your meetings, you should always let everything be done to build up the church family. Whether you share a song of praise, a teaching, a divine revelation, or a tongue and interpretation, let each one contribute what strengthens others.

- In First and Second Corinthians, the Lord used the congregation in all the gifts of the Spirit.
- The apostles, prophets, pastors, teachers, and evangelists were not the only ones used.
- Paul did not even address the fivefold ministers in his letters; he was talking to the congregation.

- He encouraged individuals to have a word, a prophecy, a tongue, an interpretation, or a psalm when they gather because everybody has something to offer.

- He taught the congregation to flow in the gifts of the Spirit decently and in order.

- Jesus spoke directly to the common people, not the Pharisees or religious leadership.

- Paul's letters to the New Testament churches were also addressed to the people.

- Paul trained Timothy, who eventually became a pastor.

- The point is that it was the Lord's heart to transfer His anointing to all believers.

- It is worth reiterating that when Jesus said signs will follow the believing ones, He was talking to everyone, not the fivefold.

- When I met Jesus, I realized that everything He did was to build up the whole body so they could minister the gospel, which includes healing.

- The fivefold ministry was never meant to do the work for the believer.

- It may come as a surprise, but it was never God's intention for ministry leaders to hear from God for the people.

- God was upset when He invited all the people He delivered from Egypt up to the mountain, and no one wanted to go (Exodus 20:18-21).

- Moses went up to meet with God and became the man of God who heard from the Lord and delivered the messages.

- Remember, that was not God's perfect will for Israel; He wanted everyone to come up.

- Today, He wants all His children to know Him and minister to others.

- When the people of Israel asked for a king, God was hurt.

- It was not originally God's will for them to have a natural king because He wanted to be their King (1 Samuel 8:1–9).

- They asked for a person to lead them, just like they asked for Moses to be the one who represented them.

- The problem is that when people put that type of pressure on kings, they had to endure many hardships (1 Samuel 8:10–20).

- Notice what Moses and King David went through when the people pressured them; both sinned (Numbers 20:9–12; 2 Samuel 11:1–27).

- If you put undue pressure on pastors or other ministry leaders to be the ones who hear from God for you, it can be detrimental; that is not God's will.

FINAL DISCUSSION:

For many, taking time to hear from God and making their own decisions seems inconvenient. We often put pressure on the government and the police when we should be making the right choices. Police officers are necessary because of the corruption in the fallen world.

Yet if we all walked in love, we would not need police because we would be honoring each other.

When people are born again, they come out of the world's system and into the kingdom of God. They may go to church, but their minds still need to be renewed; many believers still operate as they did before they were saved. If you place people in leadership before their character is developed, they will operate according to how they were taught in the world. Believers must learn how to function in the kingdom of God according to the Scriptures. The church must be taught that we all have the ability to pray for the sick (James 5:16).

Even though there are many methods by which people receive healing, all the gifts of the Spirit are available to everyone in the congregation as the Spirit decides (1 Corinthians 12:7–11). We must understand that the new covenant includes healing. Even if the gifts of the Spirit, such as miracles and healing, are not operating at the time, we can pray for people with simple faith and believe that they will receive their healing. God is bringing His church back to operating in child-like faith, according to His Word.

First Corinthians 14:26 encourages every believer to contribute to the church body. How can modern churches create an environment where all members are empowered to use their gifts?

Why do many believers still rely on pastors and church leaders to hear from God for them, rather than seeking God directly? How can this mindset be changed?

What steps can you take to grow in hearing God's voice for yourself and ministering to others with confidence?

CHAPTER 9

JESUS'S MINISTRY THROUGH US

At Lystra a man was sitting who had no strength in his feet, lame from his mother's womb, who had never walked. This man was listening to Paul as he spoke, who, when he had fixed his gaze on him and had seen that he had faith to be made well, said with a loud voice, "Stand upright on your feet." And he leaped up and began to walk.

—Acts 14:8–10 NASB

DISCUSSION:

We have discussed different modes of operation God has used to heal people, and how supernatural manifestations happened as the result of people's centurion type of faith. We will continue to talk about the insights the Lord has shown me concerning healing. When the apostle Paul was ministering in Lystra, a man who was lame from birth was sitting there, listening to him as he spoke. It is essential to notice that when Paul was teaching, he fixed his gaze on the man and discerned that faith arose in him. When he told him to stand up on his feet, he began to walk and even leaped; this is another instance of someone receiving a miracle without hands being laid on them.

As Jesus's followers walked with God and progressed through the book of Acts, their shadows began to heal people. Their words also brought healing to people. Laying on of hands and anointing with oil were not the only methods. It was far beyond what we see today.

VIRTUE OF HEALING

❖ <u>Acts 19:11–12 NASB:</u>

God was performing extraordinary miracles by the hands of Paul, so that handkerchiefs or aprons were even carried from his body to the sick, and the diseases left them and the evil spirits went out.

- Virtue went out from Jesus, and people were healed.
- Sometimes, He did not pray for them or say a word, but the power came out from Him; if people tapped into it, they received healing.
- This started happening with the apostles, as well.
- Paul was not one of the original twelve with Jesus but later became one.
- In the book of Acts, we see miracles happening through him, even though he was not one of the original.
- The church's impact kept extending out further.
- Eventually, ordinary believers worked miracles and ministered healing to people, not just those looked up to as influential leaders.
- Remember that in the book of Acts, Stephen was one of those people who extended past the apostles.
- He was not an apostle but just a regular person who had notable miracles manifest in his ministry (Acts 6–7).

Acts 28:8–9 NASB:

And it happened that the father of Publius was lying in bed afflicted with recurrent fever and dysentery; and Paul went in to see him and after he had prayed, he laid his hands on him and healed him. After this had happened, the rest of the people on the island who had diseases were coming to him and getting cured.

- Paul laid hands on Publius's father, and he was healed.
- As a result of that one miracle, people from all over the island who had diseases came to him, and they all were cured.
- As we previously discussed, this was a domino effect and continued through the book of Acts.

1 Corinthians 12:7–11 NLT:

A spiritual gift is given to each of us so we can help each other. To one person the Spirit gives the ability to give wise advice; to another the same Spirit gives a message of special knowledge. The same Spirit gives great faith to another, and to someone else the one Spirit gives the gift of healing. He gives one person the power to perform miracles, and another the ability to prophesy. He gives someone else the ability to discern whether a message is from the Spirit of God or from another spirit. Still another person is given the ability to speak in unknown languages, while another is given the ability to interpret what is being said. It is the one and only Spirit who distributes all these gifts. He alone decides which gift each person should have.

- Paul talks about the gifts of the Spirit in his letters to the Corinthian church.
- Those he ministered to were also operating in the gifts of the Spirit.

- As mentioned, his letters did not address the pastor or the fivefold, but rather the congregation.

- He essentially told them, "Listen, whether you're aware or not, the Spirit has distributed gifts to each of you as He wills."

- The gifts of the Spirit are still in operation today. Some have been given the gift of words of wisdom.

- Others have knowledge through the Spirit. Some of you have the gift of faith, and others have the gift of healing.

- The same Spirit distributes the gifts, but each person has different ones.

- The progression of Jesus's transference went from Him to the twelve, to the seventy, to the 120, and to Paul and all the apostles.

- Then, we see the transference to the congregations who received the apostles' letters.

- Remember, all the letters were written to believers in churches, and were not addressed to the pastor or leaders.

- Sometimes, Paul mentioned other apostles in his letters and named specific individuals prophets. In some of his writings, he also speaks of churches having elders and deacons (1 Timothy 3:1–13, 5:17–21).

- Notice that Paul did not say the pastor has these nine gifts of the Spirit, nor did he say apostles or prophets operate in them all.

- In these Scriptures, he was talking about the whole body of Christ.

- In 1 Corinthians, he addresses doctrine that levels the field to where everyone is in ministry; this is really the ministry of Jesus that the Holy Spirit is carrying out through us.

Acts 14:8–10 describes how Paul discerned that a lame man had faith to be healed just by looking at him. How does this demonstrate the connection between faith and healing?

____

____

____

____

____

Acts 19:11–12 shows that healing power was transferred through handkerchiefs and aprons from Paul. What does this teach us about the different ways God can work miracles?

____

____

____

____

____

Paul's letters were written to the entire church body, not just leaders. How does this challenge the idea that only certain people are called to operate in spiritual gifts?

____

____

____

____

____

THE GREAT COMMISSION

❖ <u>Mark 16:17–18 NASB:</u>

These signs will accompany those who have believed: in My name they will cast out demons, they will speak with new tongues; they will pick up serpents, and if they drink any deadly poison, it will not hurt them; they will lay hands on the sick, and they will recover.

- Mark 16:17–18 seals up the truth that we are all called to ministry.
- Jesus did not mention any leader, the synagogue, the temple, or any Pharisees or priests.
- He did not mention the disciples.
- He addressed those who believed, promising that signs would accompany them.
- "Those who believe" refers to anyone who believes—that is you and me.

- We do not have to have a special designation; we just have to believe.

- Jesus said that in His name, we will cast out demons and speak with tongues; if we encounter a snake or accidentally drink poison, it will not hurt us.

- Those who believe will lay hands on the sick and they will recover, period.

- Jesus had already declared this promise, so it could not be taken back.

❖ **1 Corinthians 12:28 NASB:**

And God has appointed in the church, first apostles, second prophets, third teachers, then miracles, then gifts of healings, helps, administrations, various kinds of tongues.

- There are several passages where Paul speaks about the gifts and functions of the Spirit.

- In 1 Corinthians 12:28, he lists apostles, prophets, and teachers.

- Then, he intermixed it with some of the gifts of the Spirit listed earlier in the chapter, such as miracles and healings.

- He mentioned helps, administration, and various kinds of tongues.

- There were many activities that took place in the body of Christ, so he summarized the different types of gifts in this passage.

- My wife, Kathi, and I were called to the gift of helps, so for years, we just assisted other ministers.

- Many people in the churches we worked for wanted us to be the head pastors, but we did not want to.
- We were called to assist the head pastor. We did not need that title or recognition to feel good or to validate our lives.
- We were willing to sacrifice to make others look good and were glad to help.
- You will not necessarily get paid to operate in your spiritual gifts.
- I encourage you to go into the marketplace and work; let the world pay for your expenses.
- Allow God to prosper you in your own business so you can pay your bills and help ministries on your time off.
- That is what Kathi and I did.
- God prospered us in our careers, allowing us more time off than usual.
- We would spend that time working at the church; we would help without expecting to get paid. We did not get paid.
- Unfortunately, these days, everyone expects to be paid.
- There is this idea that a full-time ministry will bring in a full-time salary.
- That is not how it started in the early church and is not the pattern we see in the Bible.
- Scripture describes using the tithe to pay for all the expenses of operating the tabernacle and temple (Numbers 18:21–25; Malachi 3:8–10).

- Therefore, it is not wrong to support ministers so they can devote themselves to prayer and the Word.
- Yet Jesus instructed His disciples to freely give what they have received from the Lord (Matthew 10:8).
- We should all be willing to minister healing and deliverance without expecting anything in return.
- That is the pattern Jesus set, which continued through the New Testament.
- Kathi and I were able to both minister and work in the marketplace.
- We do not have children, but we have been busy all our married life for over thirty years now.
- We have never had any time where we were doing nothing.
- Since we have known each other, we have been pursuing God and working. I encourage people to be like Paul, who both worked and ministered (1 Corinthians 9:14–16).
- That way, he could not be manipulated or controlled.

KEY POINTS:

- Certain aspects of the Christian life, such as financial stewardship, may not seem to relate to healing, but they actually do.
- We are not seeing the level of supernatural ministry that Jesus and the Holy Spirit prophesied would happen in these last days.

- We are supposed to regularly see miracles, signs, wonders, healing, and deliverance.
- We are not having the impact we should because we need to return to the biblical pattern the apostles set up.
- We must return to the simplicity of the early church.

First Corinthians 12:28 lists various gifts, including apostles, prophets, miracles, and helps. How does this passage show that every believer has a role in the body of Christ, even outside of traditional ministry positions?

Jesus instructed His disciples to freely give what they received from the Lord (Matthew 10:8). How can believers today apply this principle in their daily lives and ministries without expecting financial gain?

Many people expect a full-time ministry to provide a full-time salary. How does the early church model of working in the marketplace while ministering challenge this mindset? How can believers balance work, ministry, and financial responsibility?

❖ <u>Acts 2:42–47 NLT:</u>

All the believers devoted themselves to the apostles' teaching, and to fellowship, and to sharing in meals (including the Lord's Supper), and to prayer. A deep sense of awe came over them all, and the apostles performed many miraculous signs and wonders. And all the believers met together in one place and shared everything they had. They sold their property and possessions and shared the money with those in need. They worshipped together at the Temple each day, met in homes for the Lord's Supper, and shared their meals with great joy and generosity—all the while praising God and enjoying the goodwill of all the people. And each day the Lord added to their fellowship those who were being saved.

- Remember that in the early church, they met in houses; they got together, ate, had fellowship, sang, and had people teach the Word of God.

- The believers prayed for each other, cared for each other, and had security in smaller groups.

- It was not until recently that the church gathered in larger congregations.
- Today, there is a corporate culture in the church.
- That is partially because our government has implemented regulations; ministries must adhere to their rules and restrictions to have tax breaks and other benefits.
- Church gatherings have started to have the feel of a corporation at times.
- When there is growth, people have to manage it, but it should not take away from the power of God to heal people and minister to people.
- We have discussed the fivefold ministry and gifts of the Spirit.
- Whether one is an apostle, prophet, or has the gift of helps, we all are servants.
- Just like we elect public officials to be servants, that is how it should be in the church.
- The establishment has become toxic because we put so much responsibility on leaders to do what we should do ourselves.

FINAL DISCUSSION:

It's worth reiterating that we are not supposed to have people hearing from God for us. We should not depend on others to feed us; this has never been God's will. The Father worked salvation out so that we can have an individual relationship with Him. Jesus opened the way for us to communicate directly to the Father (Ephesians 2:18). We receive guidance and instruction from the Holy Spirit. The fivefold ministry brings unity and maturity to us as a body. It was never meant for us to minister as individuals.

The Lord has planned many miracles that will manifest in our lives. We are going to be healed and receive breakthroughs. When that happens, it will have a domino effect. God will begin moving upon us but then remember to turn outward and minister to others.

Acts 2:42-47 describes how the early church functioned in smaller, close-knit gatherings. How does this model compare to modern church structures, and what can we learn from it?

____

____

____

____

____

Why is it important for believers to take personal responsibility for their spiritual growth rather than relying solely on church leaders? How can we ensure a balance between receiving guidance and developing our own relationship with God?

____

____

____

____

____

CHAPTER 10

REACHING UNITY AND MATURITY

This will continue until we all come to such unity in our faith and knowledge of God's Son that we will be mature in the Lord, measuring up to the full and complete standard of Christ.
—Ephesians 4:13 NLT

DISCUSSION:

In this book, we have discussed dynamics that can hinder or help people receive healing. The way the church operates and relates to circumstances in the world affects the working of the Spirit. The Father's will is that the body of Christ would be unified; as believers gather together, the church should be moving toward maturity. Paul taught that the fivefold ministry and the gifts of the Spirit are designed to build up the body to reach the complete standard of Christ.

A church congregation is supposed to grow. Growth does not always refer to numbers; it applies to spiritual development and the effectiveness of producing fruit. When you meet Jesus in Heaven, you will have an audit. You will receive rewards for what you have done with what you were given. You are not responsible for what you were not given. However, the Lord expects you to produce a return on what you were given.

Compared to how it is in Heaven, our consciousness about life down here is foggy. We do not seem to discern what is most important. When you meet Jesus in Heaven, you will see clearly. You will realize what God placed in you and see what you could have done.

He will show you all the people you were supposed to help and the opportunities you did not take. In a flash, you will see what God sowed into you and that your potential was beyond what you could even record in a book.

When I went to Heaven, I realized there was so much more available than I discerned, but I was responsible for it. It is difficult to understand what you should do in this life, who you are supposed to be involved with, and the gifts inside you. It is a challenge to discern if the people around you are for or against you. Many wonder, *What relationships should I have? Which ones should I sever?* We continuously have to battle for our finances and relationships. We are fighting sickness and disease constantly. Demonic forces continually oppose us. All these issues grab our attention.

❖ **Isaiah 53:4–5 TPT:**

> Yet He was the one who carried our sicknesses and endured the torment of our sufferings. We viewed Him as one who was being punished for something He Himself had done, as one who was struck down by God and brought low. But it was because of our rebellious deeds that He was pierced and because of our sins that He was crushed. He endured the punishment that made us completely whole, and in His wounding we found our healing.

- When you stand before Jesus, the only thing that matters is what you did with what you were given.
- Although this truth is in the Bible, you may think, *Can it be this simple?*
- The answer is yes. It is actually that simple.
- When you meet Jesus, you will see He suffered, took stripes upon His back, and died so you can be healed.

- You will realize that there was never a time when you could not be healed or delivered.
- There was never a time when you were supposed to be poor or lacking financially.
- You will understand He provided a solution and a way out of everything.
- When you get to Heaven, you will realize that you suffered for choices you made and that God had nothing to do with it.
- Even though it is challenging, we must discuss this topic because it will happen anyway.
- The Word of God is accurate, and everything the Bible says about Jesus is true.
- You must reconcile with these truths, or you will not be able to bear the fact that you could have done more once you see this.
- I experienced my audit in Heaven but was given another chance to do it right. Jesus told me, "Now you have the answers. Now you can pass the test."
- I returned with the insight of how to do it right and realized that very few people have ever had that experience.

❖ <u>Ephesians 3:20 TPT:</u>

Never doubt God's mighty power to work in you and accomplish all this. He will achieve infinitely more than your greatest request, your most unbelievable dream, and exceed your wildest imagination! He will outdo them all, for His miraculous power constantly energizes you.

- To understand what is going on with me and with Warrior Notes, you must realize that I met the Healer.

- I met the person who can heal you on the spot with one word.

- I realized that nothing is impossible for Jesus. You will not tell Him, "That's impossible."

- There is nothing that He cannot do. He is able to do anything above and beyond what you can even ask or think.

- He can heal you, set you free, and resolve your finances. Sometimes, He chooses not to break through instantly because He desires to work with you to make your transformation permanent.

- He wants you to turn and help other people.

- The Lord sometimes delivers us out of situations through a process so that we learn and can help others.

- In the natural realm, most things are not instant.

- For example, if you did not get into debt overnight, it may take some time to get out of debt.

- Likewise, healing is sometimes a process that happens over time.

- God is willing to help you, but in order to receive it, you will have to work with Him.

- For fifteen years after I returned from Heaven, it was challenging to adjust to the discrepancies between what I experienced with Jesus and how it was on the earth, as I mentioned.

- The reality of how it was meant to be was apparent.
- This was the question: *How do I make the transfer to encounter the reality I saw?*
- The process should not have taken as long as it did.
- I explained that it is not easy for ministers with supernatural encounters to work their way back into this world.
- Many become ineffective and do not continue on their path because of how hard it is to deal with the discrepancies.
- The disciples became apostles because they worked with God.
- The Lord confirmed His favor on their lives because they were obedient to preach the good news of the gospel.
- They were faithful in teaching about the kingdom of God, which instilled faith in people.
- Those who heard their teachings were grounded in the truth, which led to their being established in authority and greater boldness.
- This built up tenacity in all the believers to stand in faith.

Ephesians 4:13 speaks of reaching unity and maturity in Christ. How can believers grow in spiritual maturity and contribute to unity in the body of Christ?

Isaiah 53:4-5 reveals that Jesus carried our sicknesses and provided healing. How does understanding this truth change the way we approach healing and deliverance in our own lives?

Ephesians 3:20 declares that God can do far more than we can imagine. How can we align our faith and expectations with God's ability to work beyond what we think is possible?

STAND FIRM AND STEP IT UP

❖ <u>Ephesians 6:13–18 NASB:</u>

Therefore, take up the full armor of God, so that you will be able to resist in the evil day, and having done everything, to stand firm. Stand firm therefore, having girded your loins with truth, and having put on the breastplate of righteousness, and having shod your feet with the preparation of the gospel of peace; in addition to all, taking up the shield of faith with which you will be able to extinguish all the flaming arrows of the evil one. And take the helmet of salvation, and the sword of the Spirit, which is the Word of God. With all prayer and petition pray at all times in the Spirit, and with this in view, be on the alert with all perseverance and petition for all the saints.

- Paul taught the Ephesians that after they have done everything to stand, they must continue to stand firm with the armor God provided so that they would see the spiritual realities come to pass.
- We all need to do the same.
- We do not need more encounters and visitations like people think they need.
- The only way my encounter changed me is that I had to accept the fact that we have failed, that we have fallen short, and that we are lukewarm.
- I had to acknowledge my need to step it up.
- Many have watched my life over the years as if it were entertainment.
- They ask, "How does all this happen? How does a person do all this?"

- Some believe so much is happening in my life because I went to Heaven.

- The reality is that anyone who went to Heaven and came back would be like this if they overcame the discrepancies.

- They would go through the same struggles of trying to implement the truth in a broken world.

- I mention this because when Jesus healed people, He had to get them to accept that God was a good God who did not make them sick.

- They had to receive the needed correction in their perspective.

- Those who received healing had to discern that Jesus fulfilled God's promise that a deliverer would come (Isaiah 61:1–2).

- They recognized Him as the Messiah who came to preach good news and heal them.

- Jesus was successful with those who discerned who He was but was rejected by those He was initially sent to.

- Jesus cried over Jerusalem, saying, "How often I wanted to gather your children together, as a hen gathers her chicks under her wings, but you were not willing" (Matthew 23:37)!

- He also said, "You did not know the time of your visitation" (Luke 19:44).

- They hung Him on a cross and killed Him. The ordinary people who were out in the fields and on farms came to Jesus; those who were poor and sick received their healing from Him.

- The crowds of people heard the good news that Jesus preached and flocked to Him.
- The establishment of the time did not provide for them in any way; instead, it enslaved them.
- We must be honest today and recognize that people feel restricted and enslaved by the government and the church.
- The message of the gospel is quite the opposite of what many are experiencing; it offers freedom and something supernatural.
- Miracles are supposed to be performed within the church because that is God's will.
- Yet if those organizations and ministries are compromised in any way, people begin the migration outside the building, just as the people went outside the synagogue in Jesus's day; this has happened many times throughout history.
- Throughout my college education, I studied church history, American history, and civics, along with many different types of courses.
- I had to take secular classes to get my degree, so I did not just take Bible courses.
- I noticed deficits in some situations because of demographics as I studied history.
- Studying the characteristics and statistics of groups of people brought interesting insights into human behavior.
- I learned about how people think and how we all have blind spots.

- We need each other in order to see clearly and to challenge us to think differently.

KEY POINTS:

- The apostles who came before us spoke the truth, yet the church has ignored much of what they said in the Bible.
- If we paid attention and implemented the whole counsel of the Word of God, it would balance us out and send us in a different direction than we are going.
- There has been an overemphasis on specific aspects of the Word, and other Scriptures have been left out.

Ephesians 6:13-18 emphasizes standing firm in spiritual battles by putting on the full armor of God. How can believers practically apply each piece of armor in their daily lives?

____

____

____

____

____

Jesus wept over Jerusalem because they did not recognize the time of their visitation (Luke 19:44). How can we ensure that we are not missing what God is doing in our own lives today?

____

____

____

____

____

The early church was known for supernatural miracles, but today many churches lack this element. What steps can the modern church take to restore the power and supernatural work of God in its gatherings?

____

____

____

____

____

THE WHOLE COUNSEL OF GOD'S WORD

❖ Acts 20:25–28:

And indeed, now I know that you all, among whom I have gone preaching the kingdom of God, will see my face no more. Therefore I testify to you this day that I am innocent of the blood of all men. For I have not shunned to declare to you the whole counsel of God. Therefore take heed to yourselves and to all the flock, among which the Holy Spirit has made you overseers, to shepherd the church of God which He purchased with His own blood.

- When I returned from being with Jesus in Heaven, I realized that the way the church was presenting God's Word was like a corrupt court case.
- If you were in court witnessing a case, then all the available information should be presented.
- There is a judge, a jury, and people presenting their evidence in court.
- A righteous decision should be made at the end, based on the information that has been presented.
- In an earthly court, you would try to figure out what is going on, who is guilty and innocent, and if there was negligence.
- If data or information was left out, it could cause the verdict to be wrong.
- If vital information was left out, it could have changed the perception of a jury or the judge.
- When I was in Heaven, I realized that there is truth in the Bible that is being ignored because it does not push the agenda of the ministers who should be presenting it.
- When I took journalism in college, I learned how to write. I realized that you could choose what they called your slant, which is your agenda.

- You could pick your goal and prove a point. You gather information, and you report to support your case.
- If you leave certain information out, you can skew it a certain way.
- You present certain facts to get a message across, but if you leave some facts out, it could change the way that people perceive it.
- This same issue has been happening in the church and must be corrected by teaching God's truth in its entirety.
- The revelation concerning healing, deliverance, and prosperity I received in Heaven was much more potent than what has been presented here.
- Jesus was far beyond how He has been portrayed.
- Unfortunately, how the church has taught God's Word has mostly been to accommodate each minister's individual views or support their situation.
- If there are people in a congregation who were hurt because they had not been healed, they often blame God.
- Instead, we should review all the Scriptures and realize that healing was provided on the cross.
- Divine health is something we are promised under the new covenant.
- We are responsible for getting to a place where we can receive healing through faith, knowing that nothing is impossible with God; you cannot blame Him.
- When circumstances do not turn out as expected, people often blame God.

KEY POINTS:

- Many have accused God of putting sickness on them when He did not do it.
- If people lose money, they think God does not want to help them financially, so they stop believing in prosperity.
- People who have given money and still do not seem to prosper have tied their giving to prosperity.
- When they do not get what they hoped for, they blame God.
- Many do not believe in deliverance because they had people pray over them, and nothing changed, or the devil came back.
- We must take responsibility to seek God in His Word and take hold of His promises.

❖ <u>Hebrews 11:6:</u>

But without faith it is impossible to please Him, for he who comes to God must believe that He is, and that He is a rewarder of those who diligently seek Him.

- Many people who are known in the Bible were determined to stand up and push through the spiritual warfare; they were tenacious.
- We are rewarded for being diligent.
- God rewarded the people in the Bible who clung to the promises in the Word of God and did not give up (Hebrews 11).
- When Jesus came, He served those in need; notice that they came to Him, He did not push Himself.

- You cannot force the truth on people who do not want to hear it.

- People in Jesus's own hometown did not receive any miracles.

- The people had the power to hinder Jesus from performing miracles because they did not believe in Him.

- They had doubt and unbelief, which hindered Jesus from performing what the Father had sent Him to do.

❖ <u>2 Corinthians 3:16–18 TPT:</u>

But the moment one turns to the Lord with an open heart, the veil is lifted and they see. Now, the "Lord" I'm referring to is the Holy Spirit, and wherever He is Lord, there is freedom. We can all draw close to Him with the veil removed from our faces. And with no veil we all become like mirrors who brightly reflect the glory of the Lord Jesus. We are being transfigured into His very image as we move from one brighter level of glory to another. And this glorious transfiguration comes from the Lord, who is the Spirit.

- You should focus on allowing the Holy Spirit to destroy unbelief and doubt in your life by establishing yourself in the truth.

- It should not have taken fifteen years to acclimate to this realm after returning from my heavenly experience.

- Seeing the personality of Jesus and the reality of God's will was so abrupt that it was difficult to deal with my environment.

- I had a hard time with people who withstood God.

- When I was in Heaven, Jesus spoke to me about individuals; when I shared His messages with them, most did not receive them.

- Very few people who I was sent to actually listened to me. To this day, they do not know that I was sent back for them.

- The Lord showed me some individuals who I did not know at the time and met later.

- They did not know me, but God sent me to them, and every single one received from me.

- Once I got past the people I already knew, years later, I met those who were strangers whom the Lord showed me in the vision.

- They all received the word without hindrance. Some of them, who were not even born again, got saved and healed.

- They received their package from Heaven.

- That is what you will deal with, the people who receive may surprise you.

- It will be the common people, the new converts.

- You will lead people to the Lord and see them receive healing and deliverance.

- These new converts will be the ones who you are called to disciple and mentor.

- This is what we are called to do.

- Many who are still in the churches are coming to the point where they will have to make a decision to go on with the Lord.
- If they do not, they will find themselves resisting the revival that will happen.
- As I studied the history of revivals and moves of God, I noticed that they often occurred outside the church.
- They happened with the youth and others with whom the church was not involved.

FINAL DISCUSSION:

Many of those we celebrate as generals and revivalists were kicked out of the church and they found themselves on the streets. Jesus was kicked out of the synagogue and preached on the hillsides instead. The process is sometimes painful but does not have to be complicated. It can be very easy.

I encourage you to go to the people you are called to—minister to those who are hungry and in need. Use child-like faith and simple language as you teach the people, and everything will be fine. You will see miracles. Do not push it on the goats. Give it to the lambs, the people who want the Lord, and those who want healing, prosperity, and deliverance. Just stick with those people, and everything will be fine.

Acts 20:27 speaks about declaring the "whole counsel of God." How can believers ensure they are receiving and sharing a balanced, full message of Scripture rather than selective teachings?

Many revivalists and leaders in church history, including Jesus, faced rejection from religious institutions. How should believers respond when they encounter resistance while sharing the gospel or standing for biblical truth?

Hebrews 11:6 emphasizes faith and diligence in seeking God. What are some practical ways believers can develop unwavering faith, even when facing unanswered prayers or delayed breakthroughs?

____

____

____

____

____

Second Corinthians 3:16–18 describes transformation as we draw close to the Lord. What steps can believers take to ensure they are continually growing in spiritual maturity and reflecting Christ more fully?

____

____

____

____

____

SALVATION PRAYER

Lord God,

I confess that I am a sinner.

I confess that I need Your Son, Jesus.

Please forgive me in His Name.

Lord Jesus, I believe You died for me and that You

are alive and listening to me now.

I now turn from my sins and welcome You into my heart.

Come and take control of my life.

Make me the kind of person You want me to be.

Now, fill me with Your Holy Spirit,

who will show me how to live for You.

I acknowledge You before men

as my Savior and my Lord.

In Jesus's name. Amen.

If you prayed this prayer, please get in touch with us at

info@kevinzadai.com
for more information and material.

We welcome you to join our network at **warriornotes.tv** for access to exclusive programming.

To enroll in our ministry school, go to:
www.warriornotesschool.com

Visit **www.kevinzadai.com** for additional ministry materials.

ABOUT DR. KEVIN ZADAI

Kevin Zadai, PhD, was called to the ministry at the age of ten. He attended Central Bible College in Springfield, Missouri, where he received a Bachelor of Arts in theology. Later, he received training in missions at Rhema Bible College, a ThD from Primus University, and a PhD from Life Christian University. Dr. Kevin L. Zadai is dedicated to training Christians to live and operate in two realms simultaneously—the supernatural and the natural.

At age thirty-one, Kevin met Jesus in Heaven, got a second chance at life, and received a revelation that he could not fail because it is all rigged in our favor! Kevin holds a commercial pilot license and is retired from Southwest Airlines after twenty-nine years as a flight attendant. He is the founder and president of Warrior Notes School of Ministry. He and his lovely wife, Kathi, reside in New Orleans, Louisiana.

Enroll for free and enjoy two free classes